# TATTOO SHOWCASE

## Edited by
## LAL HARDY

**ROBINSON**

Constable & Robinson Ltd
55-56 Russell Square
London WC1B 4HP

First published in the UK in 2012 by Robinson,
an imprint of Constable & Robinson Ltd

A copy of the British Library Cataloguing in Publication Data is available from the
British Library

ISBN 978-1-78033-022-8

Designed by D23, London

Printed and bound in the EU

# Contents

# Introduction

**'Tattoo' – a word, pardon the pun, that leaves a lasting impression, whether this impression be on the skin of the 'tattooed' or in the mind of whoever sees the tattoo. The fact is that tattoos have been and remain a constant source of fascination for many people, both tattooed and non-tattooed.**

As a practitioner of the ancient and intriguing art of dermagraphic embellishment for nearly thirty-five years, I have witnessed enormous changes within the tattoo world. These changes range from ready-mixed colours and pre-sterilized needles to a myriad of tattoo websites and, most strikingly from the wearer and tattoo aficionados' points of view, amazing artwork on the skin that has pushed the boundaries of artistic tattooing ever forward.

Back in the early days of my tattooing career, the tattooist would mix his own colours which were available in powder form. The powders were mixed in various solutions that included Listerine mouthwash, glycerine, distilled water, Polish vodka and washing-up liquid. Nowadays, an array of ready-mixed and sterilized colours is available. Needles used to come in packs of 1000 and the artist had to be able to create groups of needles by tying or soldering needles together. Today this laborious procedure is circumvented by needles being supplied in blister packs, sterilized and in an array of configurations to suit the procedures for which they are required.

*Below:* Japanese master Horiyushi at work.

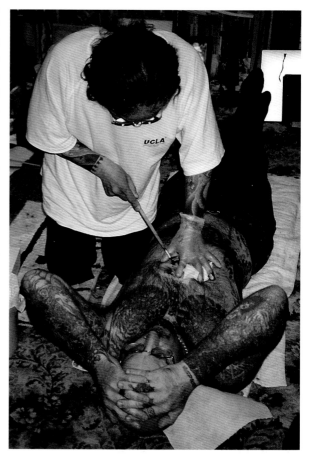

The tattoo trade back in the day was a secret society, wary of outsiders, a cloak-and-dagger world often shrouded in an aura of paranoia and (in some cases) violence. Tattoo designs known as 'flash' were the staple diet of the tattoo clientele in the early days of modern western-style tattooing with images of love, death, romance, humour, military and naval iconography the most popular. The traditional images of the tattoo as seen on older generations were quite often just re-hashes of the designs that had been wheeled out for years. One man credited with spreading the popularity of the stock tattoo design was Lew Albert. Born in the late 19th century, 'Lew the Jew', as he was known, was a former wallpaper designer who had learned the art of tattooing. Working at one time with the world-famous Charlie Wagner, Albert took it upon himself to redraw much of the flash of the time as he deemed many of his rivals' work to be of poor quality.

*Above:* A tattooed Dyak warrior in Borneo.

Albert's flash was, in turn, marketed to tattooists and for generations the designs were passed down from tattooist to tattooist, sometimes re-drawn with the artist's own take, but ultimately the same basic subjects endured.

By the mid-1970s, a new tattoo movement had begun to take place in the USA, featuring the talents of Jack Rudy, the Dutchman, Bob Roberts, Goodtime Charlie, Mike Malone, Leo Zulueta and, most importantly of all in my opinion, Don Ed Hardy. Hardy promoted tattooing through his magazine, *Tattoo Time* and various other publications from his company, 'Hardy Marks'. He was also the subject of films such as *Signatures of the Soul*, narrated by Peter Fonda, and *Ed Hardy Tattoo the World*.

Tattooing in its earliest form would have been performed with sharpened bones, tusks, teeth or sticks rather than modern electric machines. Some forms of traditional hand tattooing still exist today in places like Borneo, Samoa, Polynesia, Thailand and Japan.

*Below left:* Tattoo machines are precision manufactured to the highest standards.

*Below right:* The machines and their needles are configured differently for different tasks.

Today's electrical tattoo machines – and they are machines not guns as some refer to them – are precision engineered to the highest standards, with air-powered machines of similar quality also available. There are two types of electric machine; the rotary, with a rotating motor; and the more familiar electro-magnetic type also known as a make 'n' break, coil, iron or vibrator. Both have their origins in the 19th century. The rotary was developed by Samuel O'Reilly from a device invented by Thomas Edison for punching embroidery patterns onto cloth and patented by O'Reilly in 1891. Three weeks later Alfred South patented the electro-magnetic machine which operated on the same principle as an old-fashioned door bell and is a common sight in most modern tattoo studios. The machines are configured differently to perform various tasks such as line work, shading or colouring.

Today tattoo studios can be found in almost every town where tattooing is legal. The image of the back-street sleazy parlour is consigned to history with modern studios vibrant and, in the main, consumer friendly. Most studios have a waiting area and a variety of separate work areas. Many also have monitor screens showing examples of their artists' work as well as portfolios full of photographs and artwork to help clients make their tattoo choice. Some studios cater exclusively for a specific style – perhaps Japanese or tribal; some are custom-only studios where the artists carry out one-of-a-kind unique tattoos; some are traditional studios working from off-the-wall flash; and some studios combine all of these elements.

The variety of tattoo websites, books and magazines provides an unbelievable design source for anyone seeking inspiration for their tattoo choice and the tattoo world has

*Above left:* The Japanese style is enormously popular nowadays. (TATTOO: LUCA ORTIS)

*Top:* Stars have become a modern tattoo fashion trend. (TATTOO: SONYA TRUSTY)

*Above:* The electro-magnetic tattoo machine works just like this old doorbell.

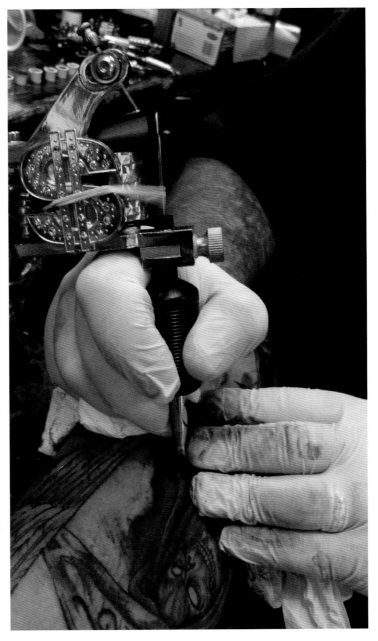

*Above:* Unique tattoos are created as specially commissioned artworks. (TATTOO: RHYS GORDON)

*Above right:* The ubiquitous electro-magnetic tattoo machine.

thrown up countless new art styles that have become immensely popular with the general public over the last twenty years. These range from dolphins and Japanese calligraphy (Kanji) armbands, to small, random tribal designs referred to in the trade as 'beach tribal' due to their popularity with beachgoers – there for all to see on a seaside holiday! Of late, star designs, script, portraits and religious imagery have become fashionable choices. The cult of celebrity has much to do with this – David Beckham's tattoos, for example, always attract media attention.

Whether you are looking for stars, a love token, an elaborate body suit, or whether you are just interested in tattoos, I hope that this book will serve to stimulate and influence you. But remember – as I tell all of my clients – you only get one hide so it pays to decide carefully about your tattoo and the artist you select to do it.

# ANGELS & DEMONS

Angels and demons, heaven and hell have been perennial favourites amongst the tattoo fraternity ever since the very first tattoo was inked. Today, the 'good versus evil' concept manifests itself in a whole range of tattoo styles and remains as popular as ever.

# Day of the Dead

The 'Day of the Dead' or, as it is know in Spanish, 'Dia de Muertos' is an ancient festival with its roots in Aztec culture. Celebrated principally, although not exclusively, in Mexico to honour dead relatives and friends, the festival takes place at the beginning of November. Many aspects of 'Dia de Muertos' have influenced tattoo art, noteably 'sugar skulls', elaborately decorated skulls made from granulated sugar .

*Above:* SAIRA HUNJAN

*Left:* MARTIN CLARK

*Opposite page*

*Top:* CHANCE KENTON

*Below left:* MATT BUTLER

*Below right:* LIANNE MOULE

Left: HANNAH AITCHISON

Below Left: DAVID CORDEN

Below middle: JOHN ANDERTON

Below right: JOE CAPOBIANCO

Opposite page

Top left: JAMES CUMBERLAND

Top right: VALERIE VARGAS

Middle left: CHRISTIAN PEREZ

Below left: NARESH BHANA

Below middle: TRACY @ HAUNTED

Below right: MATT PERRY

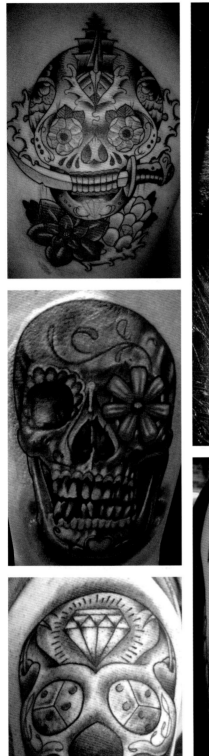

*Top left:* MARC FAIRBURN

*Top right:* LUCY PRYOR

*Left:* JULIO RODRIGUEZ

*Opposite page*

*Top left:* RODNEY RAINES

*Top right:* CECIL PORTER

*Below left:* CHRISTIAN PEREZ

*Below right:* CHRISTIAN PEREZ

# Deities

Deities are supreme beings recognised by their followers or believers as being holy, divine, spiritual, immortal or sacred. Within tattoo design, images of Eastern and Asian deities are very popular even, in some cases, with clients who have absolutely no belief in the deity they wear upon their skin!

*Opposite page:* VALERIE VARGAS

*Above:* HANNAH AITCHISON

*Above middle:* ERIC MERRILL

*Above right:* MICK TOMO

*Right:* MARC FAIRBURN

*Below:* RODNEY RAINES

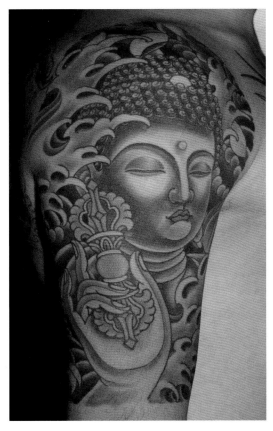

*Above:* HENNING JORGENSEN

*Above:* RHYS GORDON

*Below:* TAS

*Below:* NARESH BHANA

# Religious

In a time when church attendances are fast declining in countries such as the United Kingdom, the popularity of tattoo imagery inspired by religion is, surprisingly, at an all-time high. Much of this can be attributed to football icon David Beckham, whose religious tattoos drew worldwide attention from the media and served as inspiration to tattoo wearers in their choice of design.

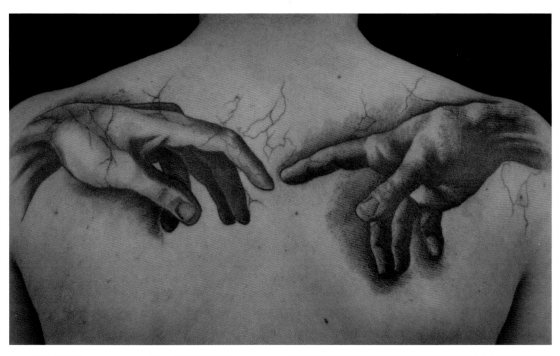

*Above:* MARK GIBSON

*Right:* STEWART ROBSON

*Below:* JASON BUTCHER

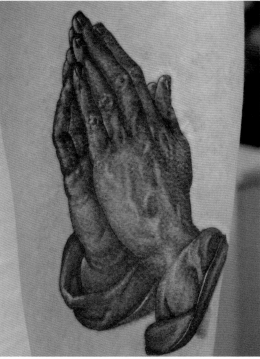

*Above:* MARK GIBSON

*Left:* MARK GIBSON

*Opposite page:*

*Top left:* MARC FAIRBURN

*Top right:* AARON SOFFE

*Bottom left:* JASON VAUGHAN

*Bottom right:* JULIO RODRIGUEZ

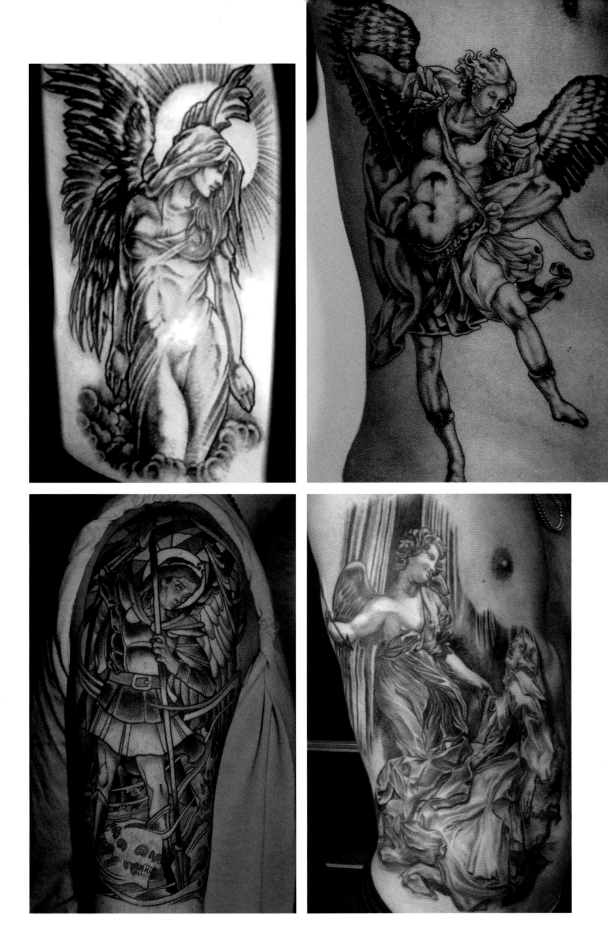

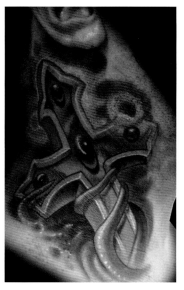

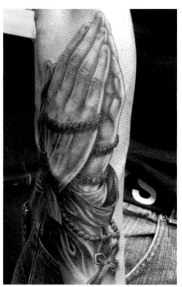

*Top left:* TOM WELLS

*Top middle:* LYNN AKURA

*Top right:* LAL HARDY

*Above left:* CHRISTIAN PEREZ

*Above middle:* LAL HARDY

*Above right:* GEMMA KAHLUA

*Far left:* WAYNE GRACE

*Left:* MATT BUTLER

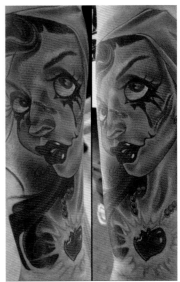

*Top left:* MATT BUTLER

*Top middle:* BOB TYRRELL

*Top right:* JO TALBOT

*Above left:* MARK B

*Above middle:* CECIL PORTER

*Above right:* JOE CAPOBIANCO

*Far right:* TOM WELLS

*Right:* TOM WELLS

*Left:* DAN ROOKE

*Below left:* LYNN AKURA

*Below:* RON KOUPAL

Nam et si ambulaver
in medio umbrae mor
non timebo mala
quoniam tu mecum es

*Top left:* CECIL PORTER

*Top middle:* KEVIN PAUL

*Top right:* MARK GIBSON

*Left:* MIREK VEL STOTKER

*Above:* ROB DOUBTFIRE

Left: KEVIN PAUL

Below left: DARRYLL RICHARDS

Below middle: LYNN AKURA

Below right: JOHN ANDERTON

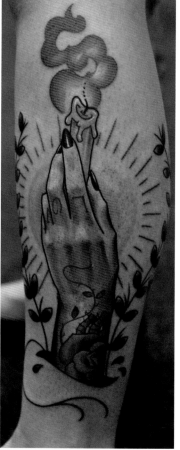

# Demons

Always a popular choice in tattooing, demons range from cutesy cartoon red devils such as 'HOT STUFF' (who appeared in *Harvey Comics*) to evil, demonic, twisted, dark, malevolent creatures. Japanese demons, known as Oni, are also fashionable, as are the ever-popular Hannya masks, used in Japanese culture to represent a jealous female demon.

*Above left:* MARK THE SHARK

*Top right:* MARK GIBSON

*Above right:* KENNY BROWN

*Far left:* HENNING JORGENSEN

*Left:* LAL HARDY

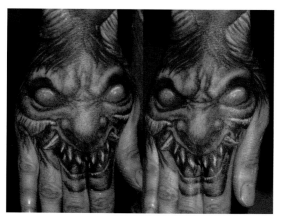

*Above:* LIORCIFER

*Right:* LEIGH OLDCORN

*Middle left:* IAN FLOWER

*Middle right:* TOR ABYSS      *Opposite page:*

*Bottom left:* STEWART ROBSON      *Top:* RODNEY RAINES

*Bottom right:* IAN FLOWER      *Bottom left:* MARK B

*Below:* HENNING JORGENSEN      *Bottom right:* HENNING JORGENSEN

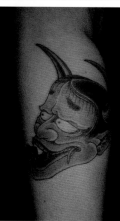

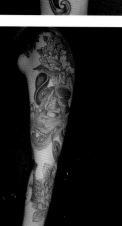

# Skulls

The representation of the human skull is universally popular in tattoo culture. It is represented and created in myriad styles from ultra realistic modern renditions to the ageless, old-school imagery. Often, old-school tattoos of the skull would be combined with wording such as 'Born to Lose', 'Like you I once was, Like me you will be', or 'Death is certain, Life is not'.

*Top:* JASON BUTCHER

*Above:* ROB DOUBTFIRE

*Left:* KORE FLATMO

Top: IAN FLOWER

Middle: CHRISTIAN PEREZ

Above right: DAN MARSHALL

Above left: CHRISTIAN PEREZ

Above right: KORE FLATMO

Right: PIOTREK TATON

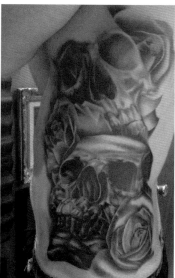

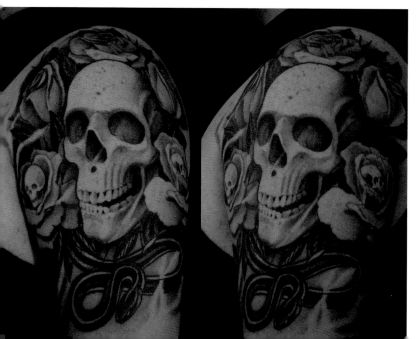

Top left: SONYA TRUSTY

Top right: ERIC MERRILL

Middle left: JOHN ANDERTON

Middle centre: MARK GIBSON

Middle right: JAMES KING

Left: KORE FLATMO

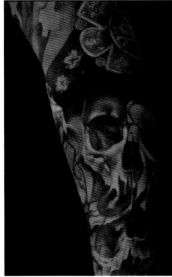

*Top:* CLAIRE REID

*Above:* CLAIRE REID

*Top right:* PHIL YOUNG

*Right:* MARK GIBSON

**Angels & Demons** 33

# WILDLIFE

Nature's wonderful array of creatures has been used in tattoo art from the earliest recorded tattoos to the present day. Totem animals, good luck symbols such as the pig and rooster tattoos found on many a sailor's feet to ward off drowning, beloved pets or creatures with which the wearer has a certain empathy – the range of tattooed wildlife is perhaps the most widely worn of tattoo imagery.

# Animals

Since they play such an integral role in the life of humans, be it as companions, pets, sporting creatures, workers, hunters or as a food source, it is not suprising that animals are found tattooed on so many people.

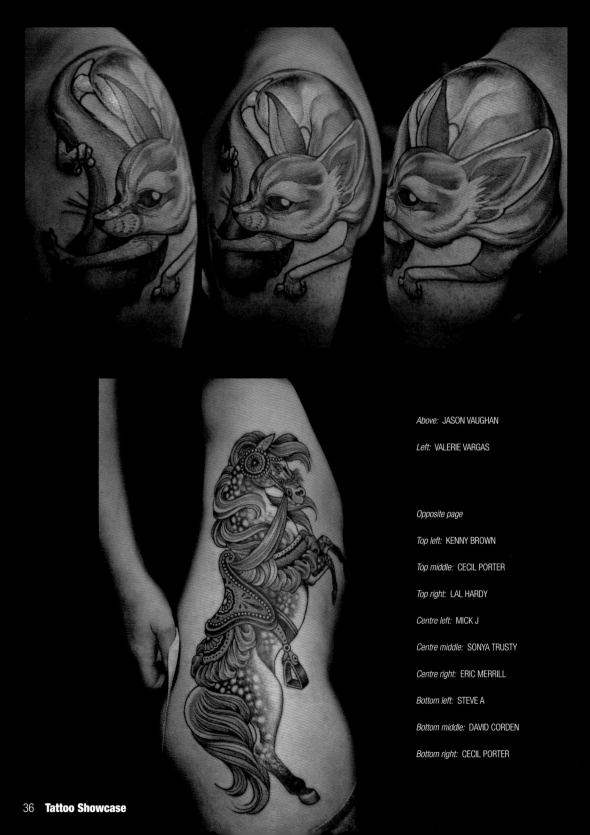

*Above:* JASON VAUGHAN

*Left:* VALERIE VARGAS

*Opposite page*

*Top left:* KENNY BROWN

*Top middle:* CECIL PORTER

*Top right:* LAL HARDY

*Centre left:* MICK J

*Centre middle:* SONYA TRUSTY

*Centre right:* ERIC MERRILL

*Bottom left:* STEVE A

*Bottom middle:* DAVID CORDEN

*Bottom right:* CECIL PORTER

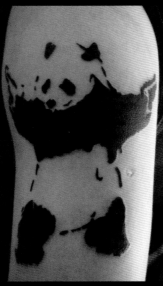

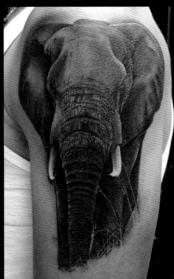

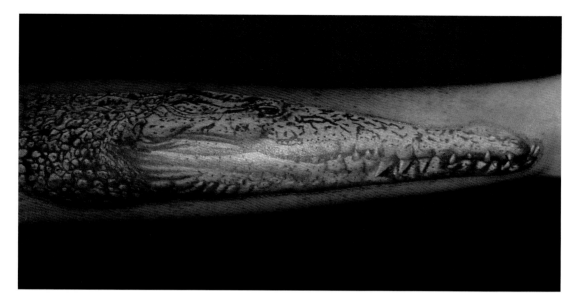

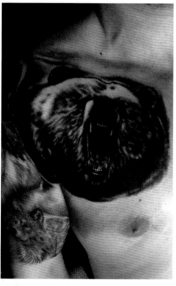

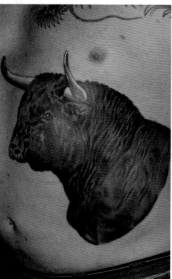

*Top:* LEIGH OLDCORN

*Above left:* KEVIN PAUL

*Above middle:* LYNN AKURA

*Above right:* JOHN ANDERTON

*Far right:* GEORGE BONE

*Right:* JULIO RODRIGUEZ

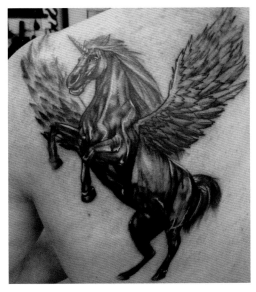

Top left: STEFANO CERA

Top right: JULIO RODRIGUEZ

Above left: JAMES KING

Above right: JASON VAUGHAN

Right: TIM HARRIS

Far right: STEWART ROBSON

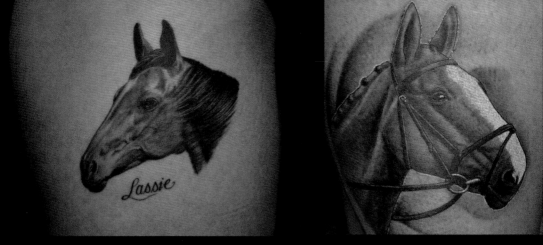

# Birds

Some of nature's most colourful creatures, birds are a constant source of inspiration for tattoo artists because of the array of colours that can be used in creating this type of tattoo. The humble swallow has been firm favourite with tattooees for generations, due, I think, to the aesthetic qualities of the design and the symbolic significance of 'flying free'.

*Below:* VALERIE VARGAS

*Below right:* TINY MISS BECCA

Top left: STEFF REIDER

Top middle: TRACY @ HAUNTED

Top right: KORE FLATMO

Above left: INMA

Above middle: NATE DREW

Above right: MARK B

Far left: INMA

Left: PHIL YOUNG

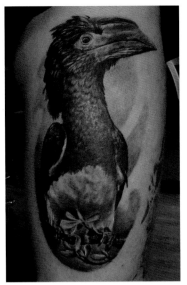

*Top left:* LEIGH OLDCORN

*Top middle:* LEIGH OLDCORN

*Top right:* MARK THE SHARK

*Above left:* LEIGH OLDCORN

*Above middle:* MICK J

*Above right:* MATT BUTLER

*Left:* NICK HORN

*Far left:* KELLEY DRAKE

*Left:* TIM HARRIS

*Below:* RODNEY RAINES

*Bottom:* ERIC MERRILL

*Above:* RHYS GORDON

*Right:* JAMES CUMBERLAND

*Below:* HENNING JORGENSEN

*Below right:* RON KOUPAL

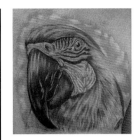

Opposite page

*Top left:* STEWART ROBSON
*Top right:* MIREK VEL STOTKER
*Bottom:* STEWART ROBSON

*Far left:* TINY MISS BECCA
*Left:* PHIL KYLE
*Above:* MICHAEL ROSE
*Below:* INMA

# Big Cats

The kings of the jungle, a symbol of pride, power and strength, lions have a long tattoo tradition, as do tigers, nature's most beautiful yet dangerous creatures. All manner of big cats are represented through tattoos. One of the most striking is the black panther, often in a crawling pose with blood-red scratches depicting where the panther is gripping its host's skin. This design was immensley popular in the early days of modern western tattooing for two reasons – its classic power and beauty as a design, and the fact that, in a time of few tattoo colours, black was the cheapest and most readily available.

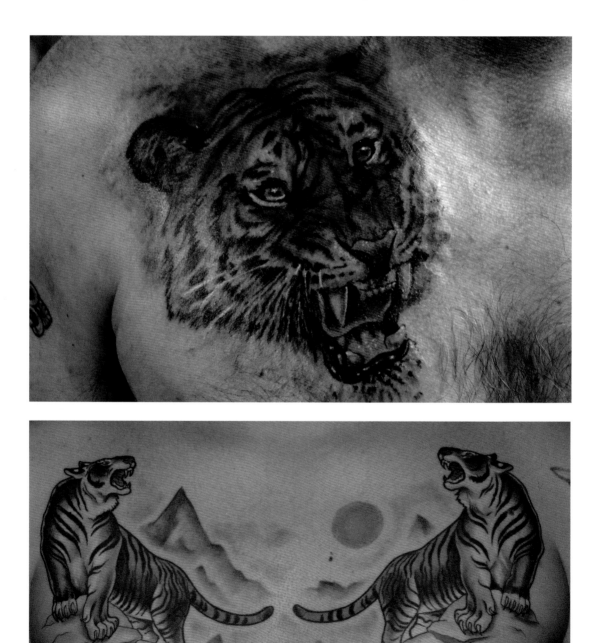

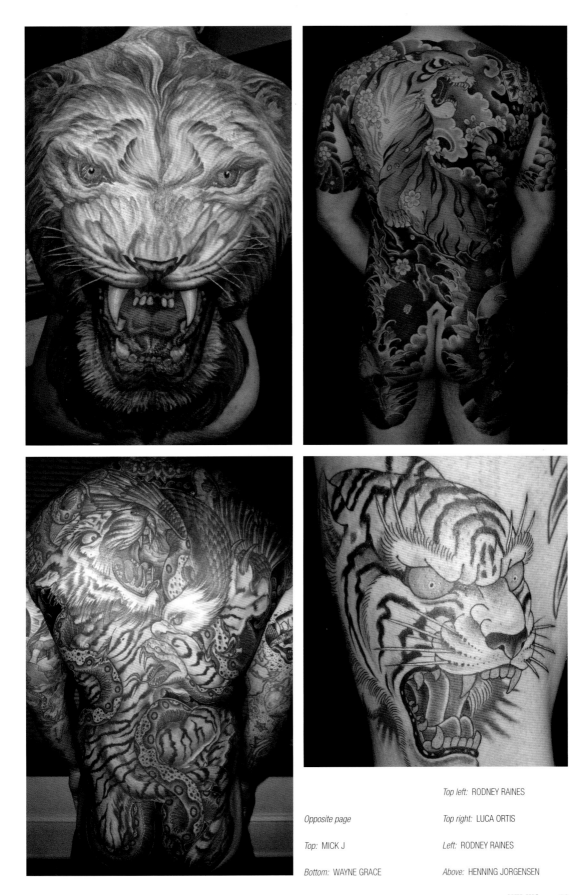

*Opposite page*

*Top:* MICK J

*Bottom:* WAYNE GRACE

*Top left:* RODNEY RAINES

*Top right:* LUCA ORTIS

*Left:* RODNEY RAINES

*Above:* HENNING JORGENSEN

Top left: KEVIN PAUL

Top right: RODNEY RAINES

Left: MICHAEL ROSE

Opposite page

Top left: LEIGH OLDCORN

Top middle: CECIL PORTER

Top right: ERIC MERRILL

Middle: JASON BUTCHER

Bottom: MICK J

Far right: DAVID CORDEN

# Creepy Crawlies

The eclectic title for this section allows us to group together images of arachnids, insects and all sorts of bugs. The spider is a common tattoo subject, as is its web, while butterflies, colorful and delicate creatures, are most popular with ladies seeking a genteel tattoo.

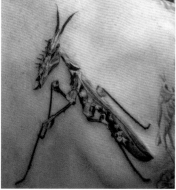

Top left: TINY MISS BECCA

Far left: DAVID CORDEN

Left: TIM HARRIS

Below left: DAVID HALL

Top right: STEWART ROBSON

Above: DAVID CORDEN

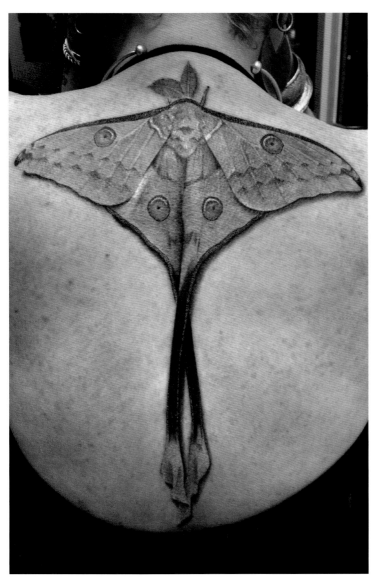

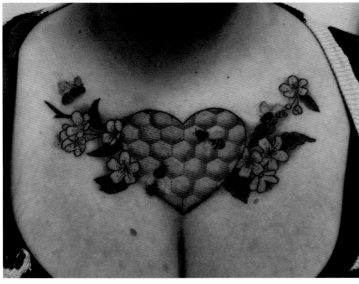

*Top left:* DAVID CORDEN

*Left:* LUCI LOU

*Above top:* CHRISTIAN PEREZ

*Above middle:* MARK B

*Above bottom:* JOHN ANDERTON

# Dogs

Man's best friend is celebrated upon thousands and thousands of dog lovers, especially in western cultures . The pet dog, *canis lupus familiaris*, is a modern-day, domesticated descendant of the grey wolf. Anyone who has owned dogs will fully understand why these loyal and faithful companions prove such a popular choice of tattoo.

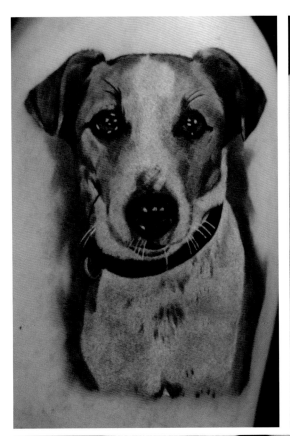

*Above left:* MICHAEL ROSE

*Above right:* MICHAEL ROSE

*Left:* MICK J

*Opposite page*

*Top left:* LAL HARDY

*Top right:* LAL HARDY

*Bottom left:* LAL HARDY

*Bottom right:* DAN MARSHALL

Top left: BOB TYRRELL

Top middle: BOB TYRRELL

Top right: MARK THE SHARK

Above left: JULIO RODRIGUEZ

Above right: TINY MISS BECCA

Far left: SILVIA Z

Left: DARREN STARES

*Top left:* MICHAEL ROSE

*Top right:* MICHAEL ROSE

*Above:* HANNAH AITCHISON

*Left:* HANNAH AITCHISON

# Eagles

Masters of the skies, these incredible birds of prey have long been seen as symbols of power, strength and freedom. They have been used on coats of arms, national flags and statues as symbols of empire. Sadly, in some political regimes the noble image has been sullied. But man's affinity with the eagle and its beauty have made it an enduring tattoo favourite.

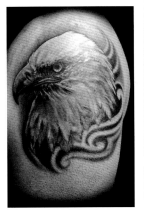

Opposite page

*Top:* JASON VAUGHAN

*Botom left:* TIM HENDRICKS

*Bottom right:* ROB DOUBTFIRE

*Above top:* STEFF REIDER

*Above bottom:* CHRISTIAN PEREZ

*Above right:* CHANCE KENTON

*Right:* TIM HARRIS

*Top:* PAUL SCARROTT

*Above:* HENNING JORGENSEN

*Above middle:* VALERIE VARGAS

*Right:* RON KOUPAL

*Far right:* DAVE BRYANT

# Koi Fish

No fish is as popular in the world of tattoo as the koi. Often very colorful in their execution, koi tattoos originated in Japan. Legend has it that, at a place called 'Dragon Gate' on the Yellow River, there was a waterfall which, if the koi could ascend it, the fish would become a dragon. For this reason, many see the koi as a symbol of strength and endurance, although many choose koi designs simply for their beautiful shapes and colours

*Top:* RON KOUPAL

*Left:* MATT BUTLER

Opposite page
Top left: NICK HORN

Top right: PAUL SCARROTT

Far left: STEFF REIDER

Middle left: STEFF REIDER

Middle right: DARREN STARES

Bottom: DARREN STARES

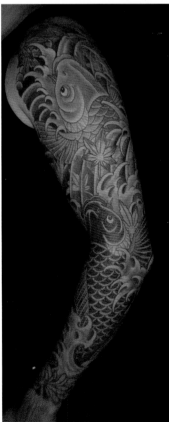

Above left: IAN FLOWER

Above right: LUCA ORTIS

Right: LUCA ORTIS

Far right: HENNING JORGENSEN

*Top left:* STEFF REIDER

*Top right:* NICK HORN

*Left:* RODNEY RAINES

*Opposite:* ERIC MERRILL

# Marine Life

Tattoos have long been associated with the sea due to their popularity with sailors and travellers. It is fair to say that voyages of discovery brought tattooing and body adornment to and from almost every corner of the world. Nautical themes, lighthouses, sultry sirens and creatures of the deep are all found adorning jolly jack tars.

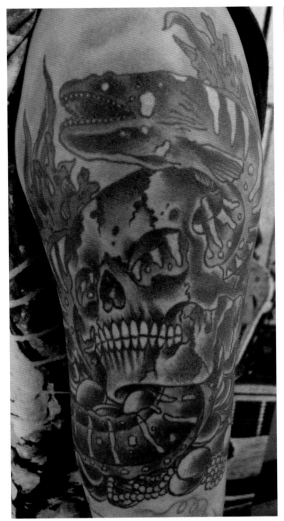

*Above:* PHIL KYLE

*Right:* MARC FAIRBURN

*Top right:* RODNEY RAINES

*Middle right:* LEIGH OLDCORN

*Bottom centre:* TIM HARRIS

*Bottom right:* GEMMA KAHLUA


*Opposite page*

*Top:* CLAIRE REID

*Far left:* ALLAN GRAVES

*Right:* RODNEY RAINES

*Below right:* CHANCE KENTON

# Owls

Solitary, nocturnal hunters of the night, owls are a strange-looking bird associated in many western cultures as being imbued with wisdom – the wise old owl. Ancient Greeks saw the owl as an omen of good luck, while the Romans saw them as a sign of disaster. Wherever owls are found, folklore surrounds them. Over the last ten years, the image of the owl has become increasingly popular as a tattoo. Bizzarely, in some cases this is due to the popularity of the Harry Potter books and films in which the hero has a snowy owl named Hedwig.

*Left:* ERIC MERRILL

*Below:* JASON VAUGHAN

*Opposite page*

*Top left:* TINY MISS BECCA

*Top right:* LUCY PRYOR

*Below:* TINY MISS BECCA

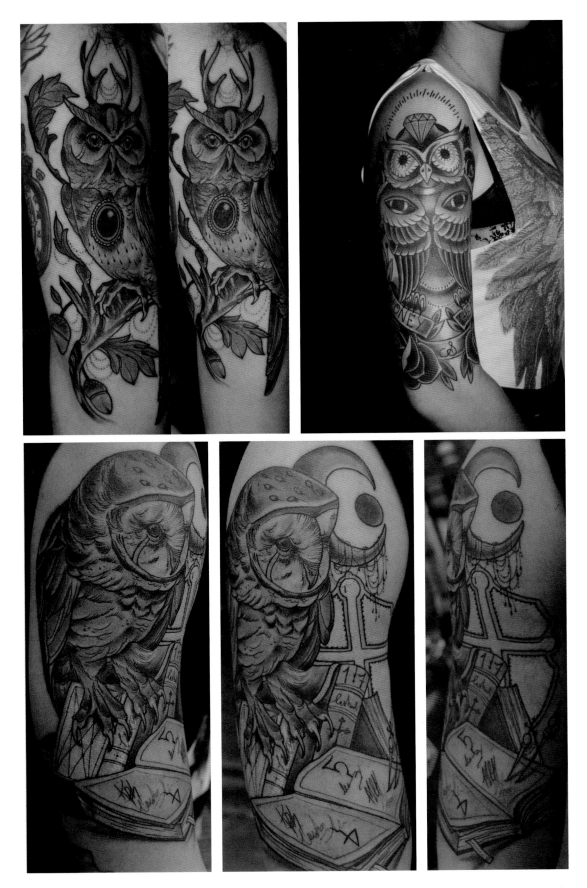

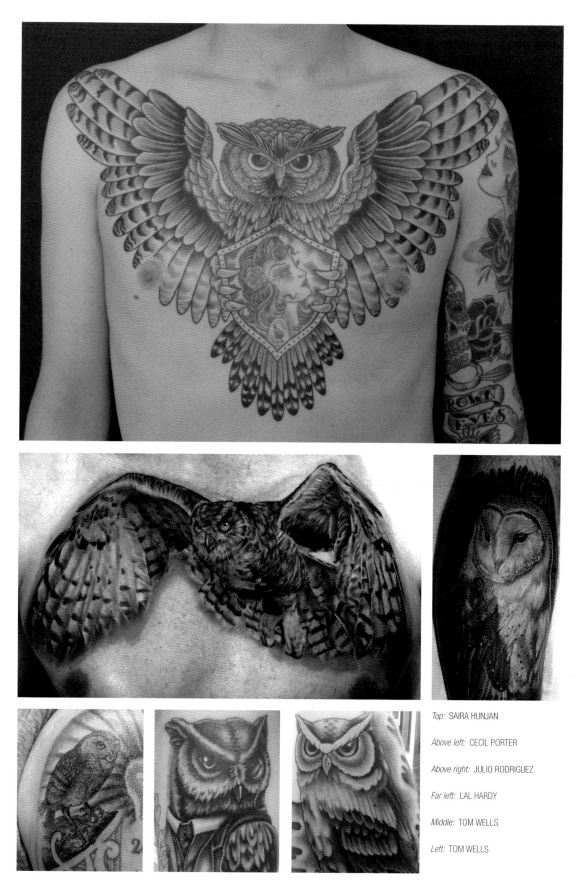

Top: SAIRA HUNJAN

Above left: CECIL PORTER

Above right: JULIO RODRIGUEZ

Far left: LAL HARDY

Middle: TOM WELLS

Left: TOM WELLS

Above: INMA

Right: CHRISTIAN PEREZ

Below left: PHIL KYLE

Below middle: CECIL PORTER

Below right: JOHN ANDERTON

# Snakes

Snakes entwined round daggers, swords, maidens and creatures are stock designs in the tattoo world. In Japanese tattooing, snakes often feature in elaborate designs and in some ancient cultures, snakes were perceived as having a diverse range of magical powers. The exotic and deadly nature of some snakes has made them iconic tattoos, none more so than the cobra.

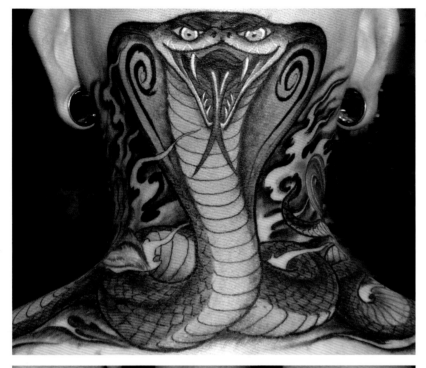

*Left:* RODNEY RAINES

*Below:* LUCA ORTIS

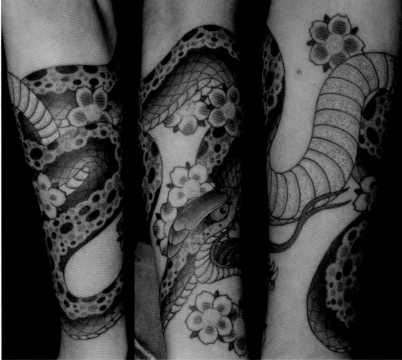

*Opposite page*

*Top left:* HENNING JORGENSEN

*Top right:* PAUL SCARROTT

*Below left* KENNY BROWN

*Below right:* MARTIN CLARK

# PEOPLE

The human form is depicted in many different ways in tattoo art, from 'the woman of my dreams'-type busty gal found on many sailors, to renditions of the famous or the infamous and ultra realistic portraits of loved ones.

# Native Americans

The images of red indian chiefs, braves and squaws have been found on tattoo design sheets from the time the earliest forms of commercial flash became available. The wisdom, teachings, bravery and, sadly, the mistreatment of the Native Americans still holds great significance in the modern age. Many people with a sympathy and empathy for the Native Americans express their feelings with tattoos.

*Opposite page*

*Top left:* PIOTREK TATON

*Top middle:* MARK THE SHARK

*Top right:* MARK THE SHARK

*Bottom left:* BOB DONE

*Bottom middle:* MATT BUTLER

*Top right:* MARK THE SHARK

*Top:* DARRYLL RICHARDS

*Left:* CHRIS HIGGINS

*Above:* MICK TOMO

*Above right:* LEIGH OLDCORN

# Portraits

Over the last ten years, and with the popularity of shows like *Miami Ink* and *LA Ink* showcasing the ability of some artists to create realistic portraiture, a trend has swept through the tattoo trade for people requesting portraits of family, friends, movie stars, comedians, politicians, musicians, murderers – you name them and someone has done a portrait of them!

*Above left:* CLAIRE REID

*Above right:* PAUL SCARROTT

*Right:* CECIL PORTER

*Far right:* CHANCE KENTON

*Below:* CECIL PORTER

*Opposite page*

*Top:* CLAIRE REID

*Below left:* CHRISTIAN PEREZ

*Below right:* CLAIRE REID

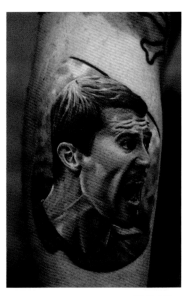

*Top left:* LEIGH OLDCORN

*Top centre:* JULIO RODRIGUEZ

*Top right:* JOHN ANDERTON

*Middle left:* TIM HARRIS

*Middle centre:* TIM HARRIS

*Middle right:* JOHN ANDERTON

*Bottom left:* LEIGH OLDCORN

*Bottom right:* LEIGH OLDCORN

# Geishas

A timeless tattoo design, the image of the geisha with flowing kimomo is commonly found in traditional Japanese tattooing as well as in traditional western tattooing where pin-up type images of these mysterious, exotic oriental ladies often adorned the arms of naval personnel.

*Right:* ELY SMYLY

*Below left:* MARTIN CLARK

*Below right:* STEWART ROBSON

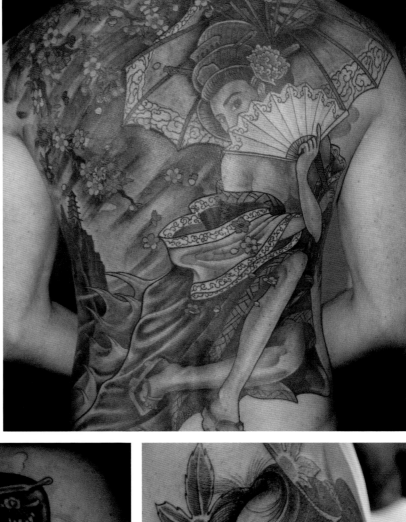

Opposite page

Left: MATT BUTLER

Top right: LEIGH OLDCORN

Second right: HENNING JORGENSEN

Third right: JO TALBOT

Bottom right: DAVID CORDEN

Above left: PAUL SCARROTT

Above right: WAYNE GRACE

Right: PAUL SCARROTT

# Eyes

Some say that the eyes are the windows to the soul. Eyes have captivated lovers, while all-seeing and evil eyes hold a peculiar kind of terror. Lately, tattoos of feminine eyes have become quite common as has the Egyptian Eye of Horus.

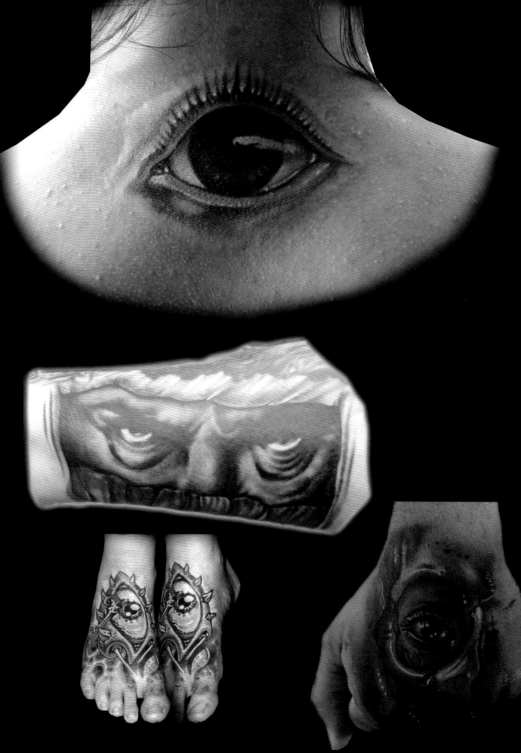

*Top left:* TOM WELLS

*Top right:* BOB TYRRELL

*Middle left:* KEVIN PAUL

*Middle right:* CHRISTIAN PEREZ

*Right:* CLAIRE REID

*Opposite page*

*Top:* CHRISTIAN PEREZ

*Middle:* KEVIN PAUL

*Bottom left:* CHRISTIAN PEREZ

*Bottom right:* JASON BUTCHER

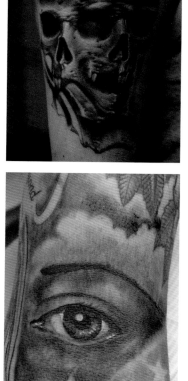

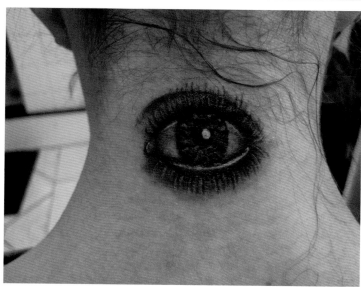

*Top left:* LAL HARDY

*Top centre:* LAL HARDY

*Top right:* PIOTREK TATON

*Middle left:* MICK TOMO

*Middle centre:* SILVIA Z

*Middle right:* LAL HARDY

*Left:* SAM JONES

# Famous Faces

In an age of celebrity, glam and glitz, it is unsurprising that fans of music and movies seek portraits of their idols, but this phenomenon within the tattoo world goes beyond showbiz images, with world leaders, martyrs and people of science all being embellished onto skin.

*Above:* HANNAH AITCHISON

*Right:* JULIO RODRIGUEZ

*Far right:* KELLEY DRAKE

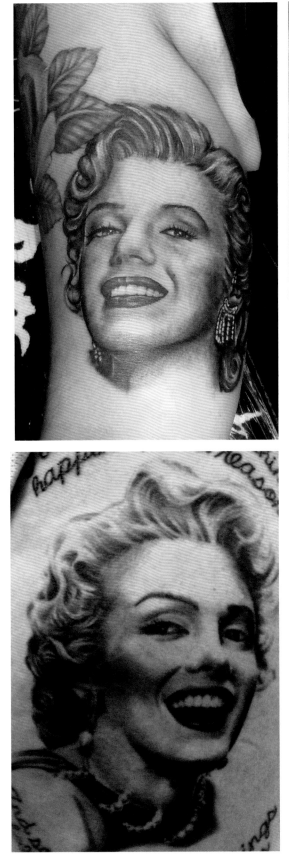

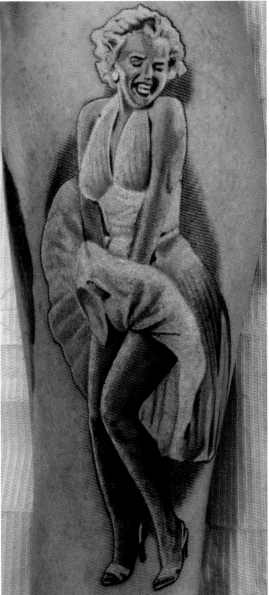

*Top left:* SILVIA Z

*Top right:* LEIGH OLDCORN

*Bottom left:* KELLEY DRAKE

*Bottom right:* MICHAEL ROSE

*Opposite page*

*Top left:* LEIGH OLDCORN

*Top right:* LEIGH OLDCORN

*Bottom left:* BOB TYRRELL

*Bottom right:* BOB TYRRELL

*Top left:* DAVID CORDEN

*Middle left:* WAYNE GRACE

*Far left:* DARREN STARES

*Above:* SILVIA Z

*Left:* BOB TYRRELL

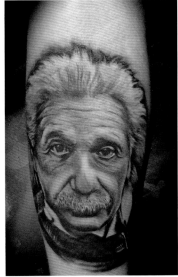

Above: PIOTREK TATON

Right: KORE FLATMO

Top right: SILVIA Z

Middle right: DAVID CORDEN

Far right: SILVIA Z

# DESIGNS
# FOR LIFE

✺

I guess all tattoos (barring removal) are, for the wearer, designs
for life, whether they consist of elaborate script, noble crowns or
geometric patterns. This section, therefore, really is a *pot-pourri*
of tattoo imagery.

# Royalty

During the Victorian and Edwardian eras, it was not uncommon for people to tattoo images related to royalty, be it the royals themselves or royal coats of arms. British royals George V and Edward VII were tattooed and this inspired an upsurge in tattooing in the UK when news of their tattooing was made public. Nowadays, images of crowns are very popular and kings and queens from decks of cards are often found as tattoo images.

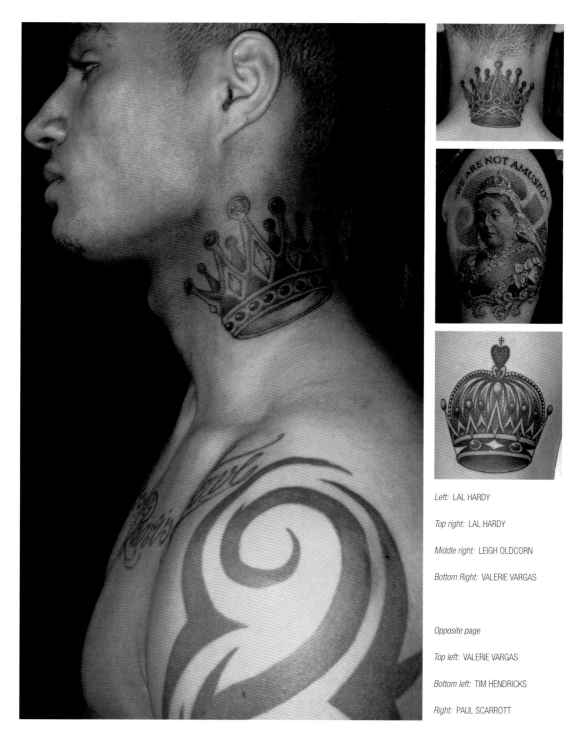

*Left:* LAL HARDY

*Top right:* LAL HARDY

*Middle right:* LEIGH OLDCORN

*Bottom Right:* VALERIE VARGAS

*Opposite page*

*Top left:* VALERIE VARGAS

*Bottom left:* TIM HENDRICKS

*Right:* PAUL SCARROTT

# Script & Writing

Writing has always been popular within tattooing. The words 'mum' and 'dad' must have been inked millions of times, but in this day and age a whole new sphere of literary tattooing can be found. Beautiful calligraphy originating in the Hispanic areas of LA is now firmly established in the tattoo world. Prayers, poems, odes, slang, slogans, sayings, verse and chapter are all found in the skin.

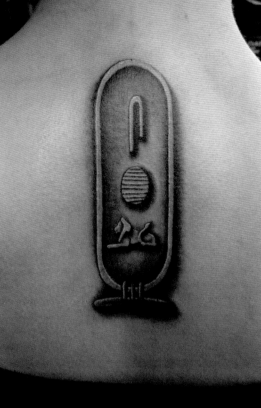

Top left: JO TALBOT

Top right: TOM WELLS

Right: SIMON ERL

Bottom right: LAL HARDY

Opposite page

Top: MARK B

Bottom: STEFANO CERA

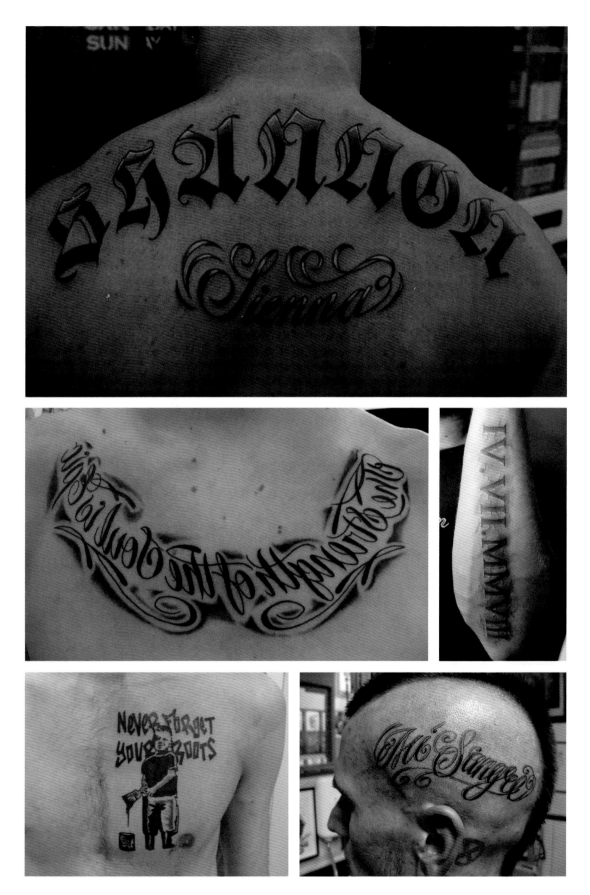

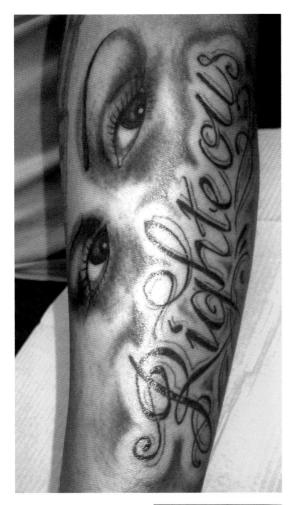

*Top left:* LAL HARDY

*Right:* SONYA TRUSTY

*Top right:* WIL PURNELL

*Second right:* KELLEY DRAKE

*Third right:* KELLEY DRAKE

*Far right:* SONYA TRUSTY

*Bottom:* CLAIRE INNIT


Opposite page

*Top:* TOM WELLS

*Middle left:* GEMMA KAHLUA

*Middle right:* WAYNE GRACE

*Bottom left:* CLAIRE INNIT

*Bottom right:* MATT BUTLER

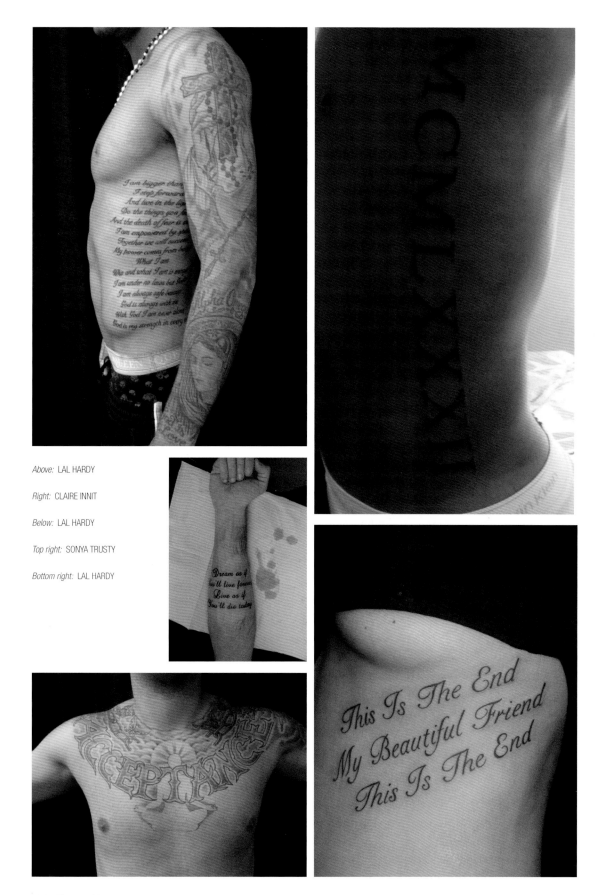

*Above:* LAL HARDY

*Right:* CLAIRE INNIT

*Below:* LAL HARDY

*Top right:* SONYA TRUSTY

*Bottom right:* LAL HARDY

# Tribal

Now one of the most requested tattoo designs, 'tribal' tattoos range from the traditional patterns of the south seas islanders to the latest interpretations in modern graphic body art.

*Top left:* DARRYLL RICHARDS

*Bottom left:* MATT BLACK

*Top right:* CHRIS HIGGINS

*Bottom right:* AARON SOFFE

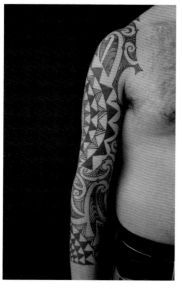

*Top left:* MICK TOMO

*Top middle:* CURLY

*Top right:* DARRYLL RICHARDS

*Middle left & centre:* MATT BLACK

*Middle right:* MATT BLACK

*Far left:* MATT BLACK

*Left:* NARESH BHANA

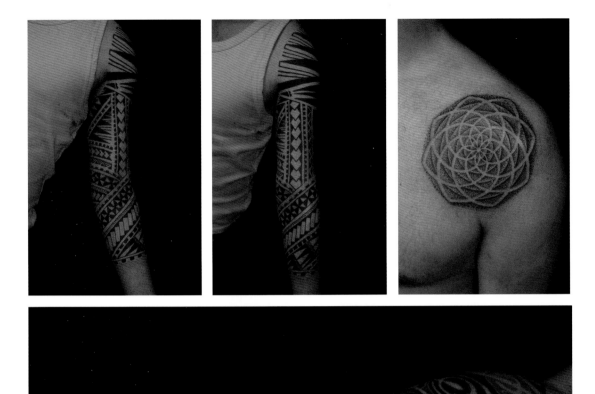

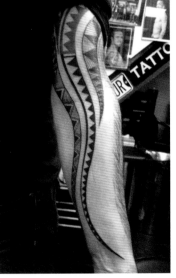

Top left & middle: MATT BLACK

Top right: MATT BLACK

Above: MATT BLACK

Right: CHRIS HIGGINS

Far right: LAL HARDY

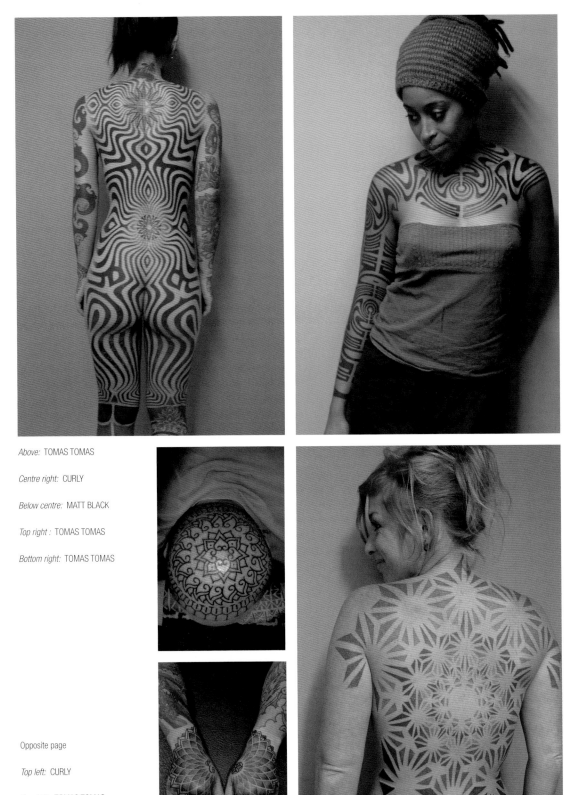

Above: TOMAS TOMAS

Centre right: CURLY

Below centre: MATT BLACK

Top right : TOMAS TOMAS

Bottom right: TOMAS TOMAS

Opposite page

Top left: CURLY

Top right: TOMAS TOMAS

Bottom left: TOMAS TOMAS

Bottom right: ALEX BINNIE

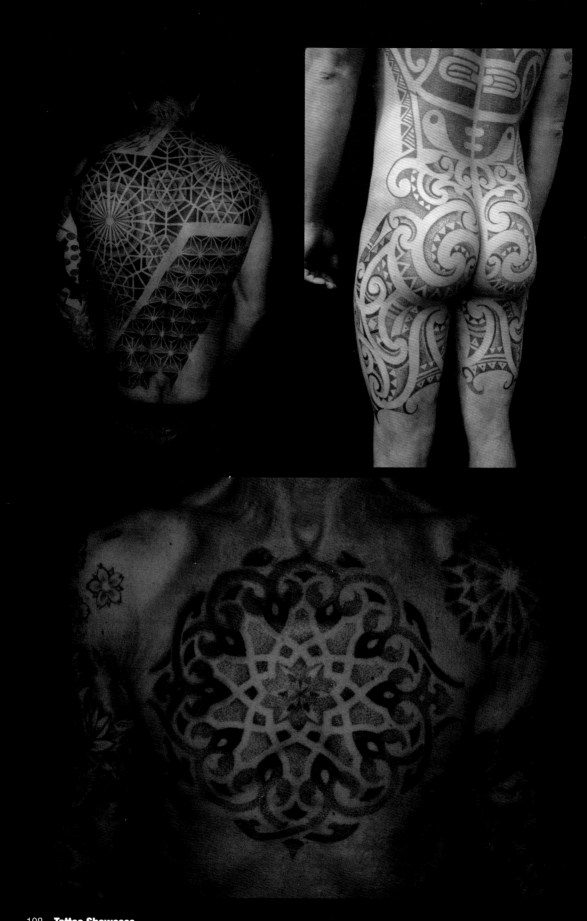

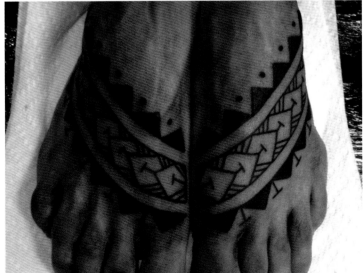

*Above:* TOMAS TOMAS

*Top right:* HARRY O

*Middle right:* MARK GIBSON

*Right:* CHRIS HIGGINS

*Opposite page*

*Top left:* MATT BLACK

*Top right:* TOMAS TOMAS

*Bottom:* MATT BLACK

*Top:* CHRIS HIGGINS

*Above:* CHRIS HIGGINS

*Left:* MATT BLACK

*Opposite:* NARESH BHANA

# Feathers

The peacock feather, due to its colourful and exotic nature, is often seen in tattooing as are feather bands based on Native American armbands.

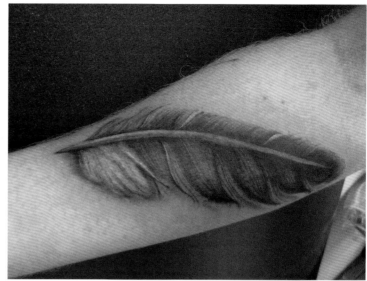

*Top left:* BOB DONE

*Above:* LIANNE MOULE

*Top right:* SAM JONES

*Right:* STEFANO CERA

*Opposite:* RODNEY RAINES

# Unusual

This section, I am sure, will raise various responses from fits of laughter to the plain question 'WHY?'

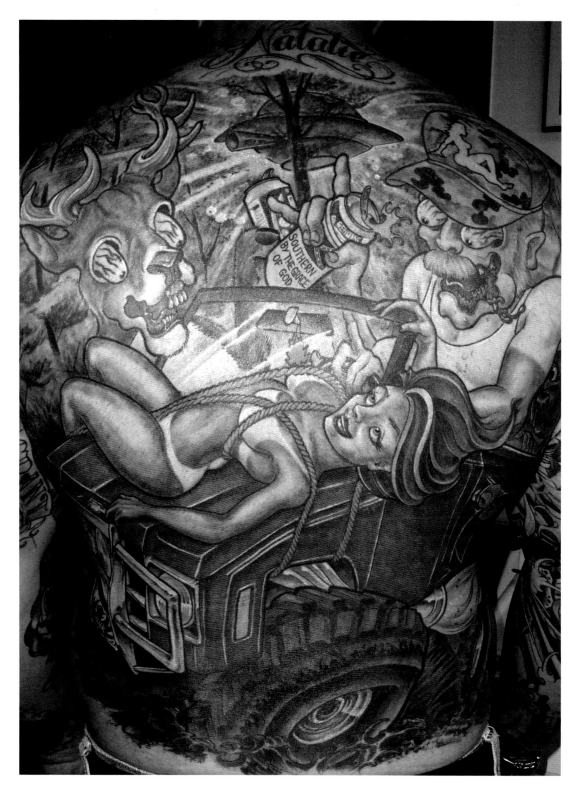

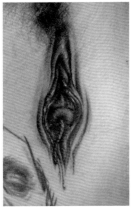

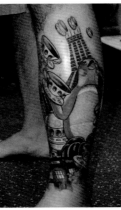

*Top left:* KENNY BROWN

*Middle left:* KEVIN PAUL

*Middle right:* JO TALBOT

*Bottom left:* JO TALBOT

*Bottom right:* CLAIRE INNIT

*Above:* PHIL YOUNG

*Opposite page*

*Top left:* DAVE BRYANT

*Top right, bottom left & right:* DUNCAN X

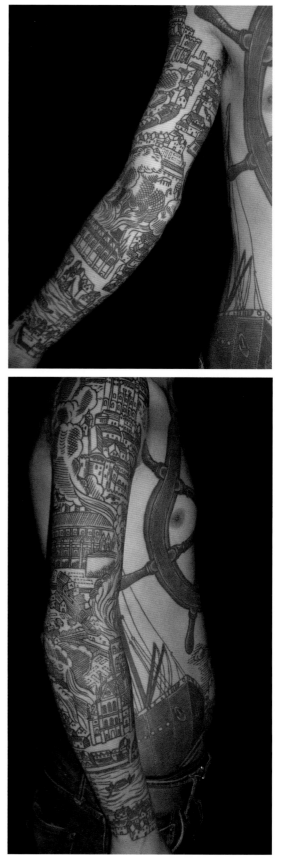

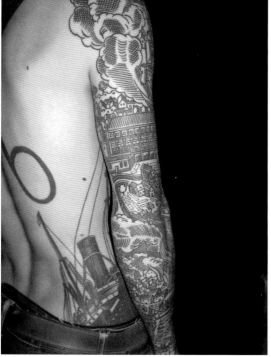

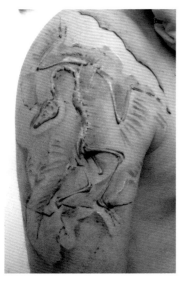

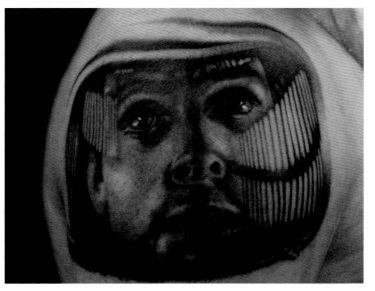

Top left: DAVID CORDEN

Above: DUNCAN X

Top right: LEIGH OLDCORN

Right: JASON BUTCHER

Opposite page
Top left: HANNAH AITCHISON

Top centre: HANNAH AITCHISON

Top right PIOTREK TATON

Middle left: LAL HARDY

Centre: MARK B

Middle right: LAL HARDY

Bottom left: MATT PERRY

Bottom right: NATE DREW

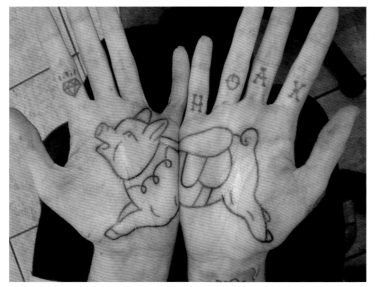

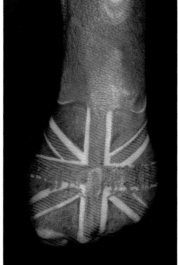

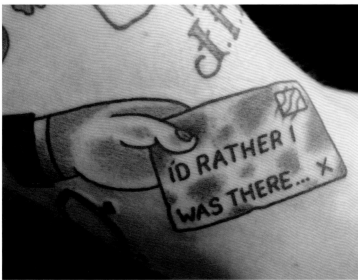

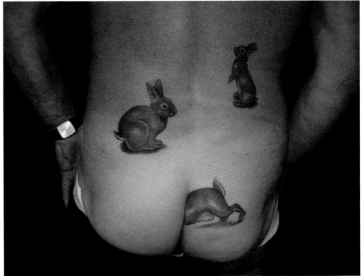

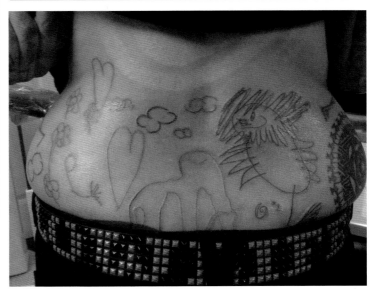

Top left: SIMON ERL

Top right: WAYNE GRACE

Above: JOHN ANDERTON

Middle right: CLAIRE INNIT

Right: TOR ABYSS

Far right: ADRIAN WILLARD

Opposite page
Top left: HARRY O

Top right: MARTIN CLARK

Middel left: LAL HARDY

Centre: LAL HARDY

Middle right: MARTIN CLARK

Bottom left: RHYS GORDON

Bottom right: JASON SAGA

# FANTASY

Who, either as a child or as an adult, has not at some time in their life been transported to a fantasy land in a dream or, perhaps, in a nightmare?

# Cartoons

Cartoons, due to their very graphic and simplistic animation, are firm favourites with the tattoo world. Cheeky humorous characters and celluloid animated stars we have grown up with are regularly celebrated in tattooing ink.

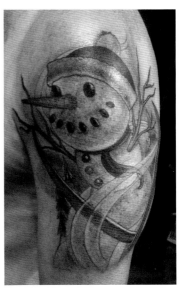

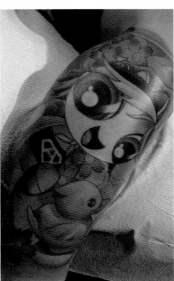

*Top left:* TOR ABYSS

*Top centre:* PIOTREK TATON

*Top right:* ERIC MERRILL

*Middle left:* ERIC MERRILL

*Centre:* JOHN ANDERTON

*Middle right:* SIMON ERL

*Right:* SIMON ERL

*Far right:* MARK THE SHARK

*Opposite:* STEFF REIDER

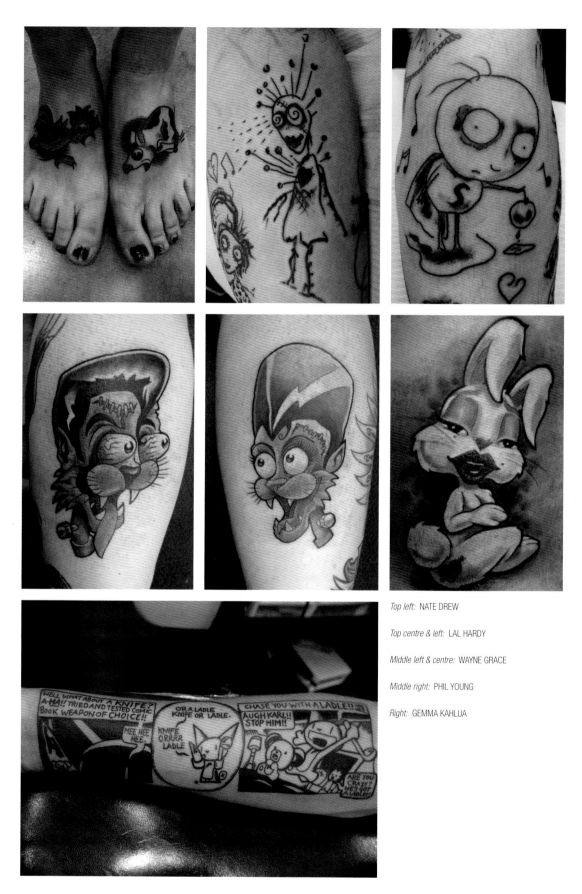

*Top left:* NATE DREW

*Top centre & left:* LAL HARDY

*Middle left & centre:* WAYNE GRACE

*Middle right:* PHIL YOUNG

*Right:* GEMMA KAHLUA

# Heroes & Villains

Like cartoons, comic book heroes and villains hold a strong place in tattooing. Often our interest in these characters starts in childhood or adolescence and progresses into adulthood. Many of the characters come from the pages of DC or Marvel comics, Batman and the Joker in their various art guises being very popular as tattoos.

*Left:* AARON SOFFE

*Below left:* PIOTREK TATON

*Below right:* LAL HARDY

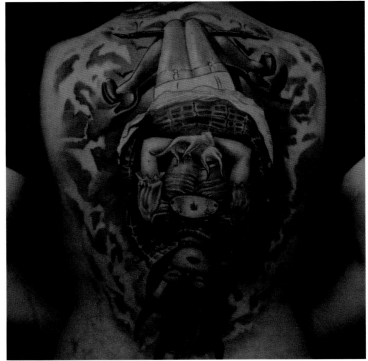

Top left: JULIO RODRIGUEZ

Top right: JOHN ANDERTON

Centre: KEVIN PAUL

Bottom left: MICHAEL ROSE

Bottom right: SILVIA Z

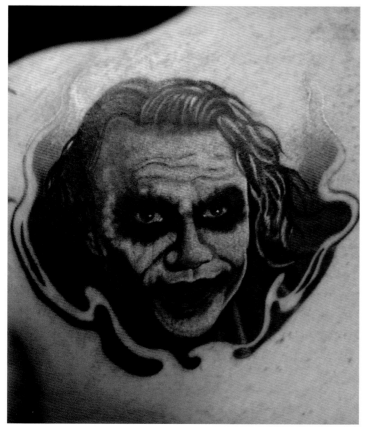

 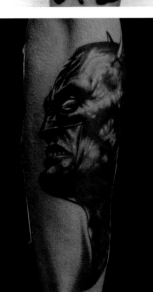 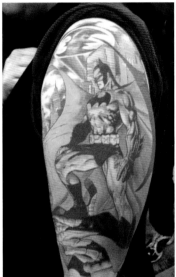

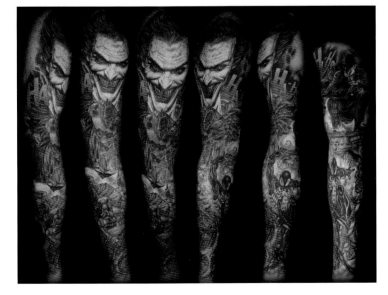

*Top left:* JAMES KING

*Top middle:* MARK B

*Top right:* JASON VAUGHAN

*Centre left:* MARK FAIRBURN

*Centre:* KEVIN PAUL

*Centre right:* JULIO RODRIGUEZ

*Left:* TIM HARRIS

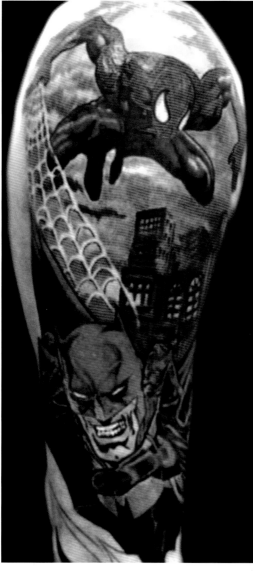

Above: MARC FAIRBURN

Above right: JOE CAPOBIANCO

Right: JOHN ANDERTON

Far right: HANNAH AITCHISON

# Pin-ups

The pin-up girl tattoo – from the classic Sailor Jerry-style, old-school pin-ups to interpretations of the masters such as Gil Elvergren, Alberto Vargas and Olivia De Beradin, to name but three – are the dream girls available to all via the tattoo. The classic military and 1950s pin-ups, as seen in numerous pulp fiction books, girlie mags and on the noses of American warplanes, are the mainstay of pin-up art in tattooing at present.

*Left:* MARK GIBSON

*Below:* HANNAH AITCHISON

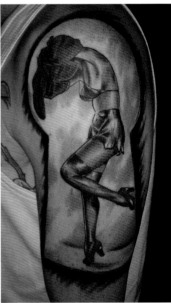

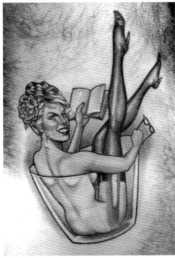

*Top left:* HANNAH AITCHISON

*Middle left:* TIM HARRIS

*Bottom left:* TIM HARRIS

*Top centre:* HANNAH AITCHISON

*Above:* MARTIN CLARK

*Top right:* TIM HARRIS

*Middle right:* MARTIN CLARK

*Bottom right:* MARTIN CLARK

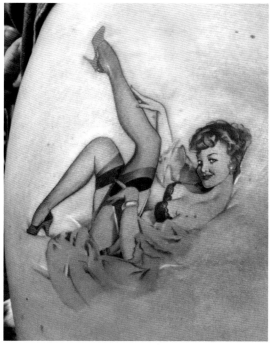

Top left: DAVID CORDEN

Top right: DAVID CORDEN

Above left: TIM HARRIS

Above right: DAVID CORDEN

Bottom left: HANNAH AITCHISON

Bottom centre: HANNAH AITCHISON

Bottom right: LEIGH OLDCORN

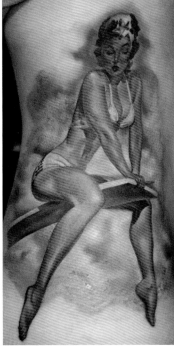

*Top left:* TIM HARRIS

*Middle left:* RODNEY RAINES

*Bottom left:* WAYNE GRACE

*Top centre:* TIM HARRIS

*Bottom centre:* JOE CAPOBIANCO

*Top right:* HANNAH AITCHISON

*Bottom right:* RODNEY RAINES

Opposite page
*Top left:* DAVID CORDEN

*Top right:* HANNAH AITCHISON

*Bottom left:* TIM HENDRICKS

*Bottom right:* HANNAH AITCHISON

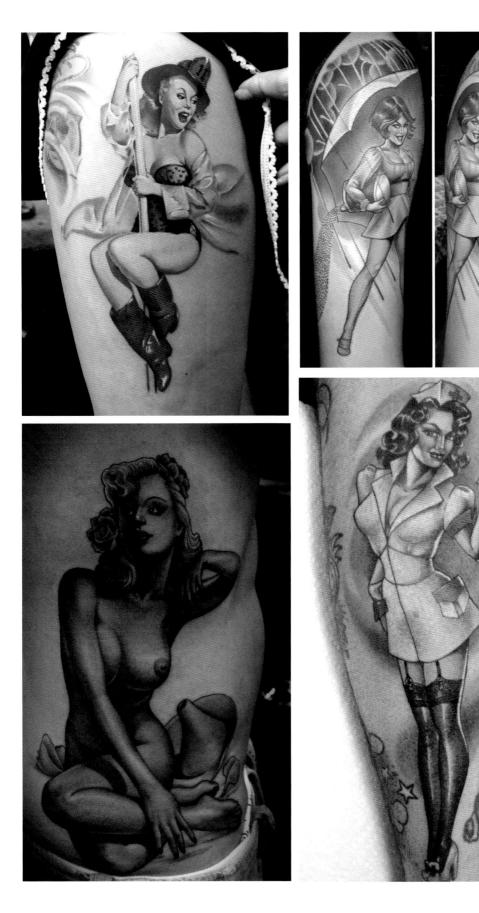

# Horror

Horror stories and horror movies have long held a fascination for many, the classic tales of *Dracula* and *Frankenstein,* immortalised in the old black and white movies and in the Hammer Horror movies, have provided endless inspiration for tattoo designs, as have zombies, ghouls and demons and all manner of things macabre.

*Top:* LIORCIFER

*Above left:* JULES @ INKERS

*Above right:* LIORCIFER

*Above left:* LIORCIFER

*Above right:* LIORCIFER

*Above:* DAN MARSHALL

*Left:* LIORCIFER

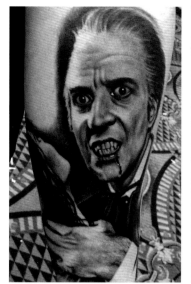

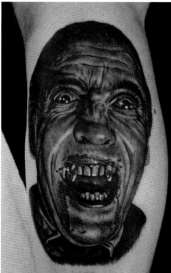

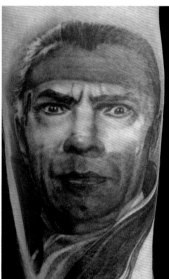

*Top left:* BOB TYRRELL

*Top middle:* DARREN STARES

*Top right:* PHIL YOUNG

*Far left:* CECIL PORTER

*Left:* PHIL YOUNG

*Below:* PHIL YOUNG

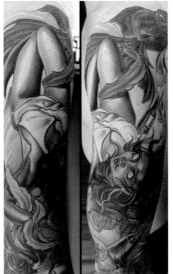

Top left: CECIL PORTER

Top right: ALLAN GRAVES

Centre left: PIOTREK TATON

Centre: MARK GIBSON

Above: LAL HARDY

Far left: LEIGH OLDCORN

Left: JOE CAPOBIANCO

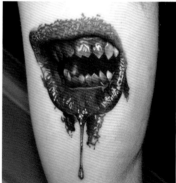

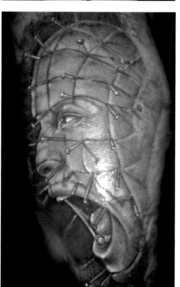

*Top left:* MIREK VEL STOTKER

*Middle left:* MATT PERRY

*Bottom left:* INMA

*Top centre:* MARK GIBSON

*Centre:* MICHAEL ROSE

*Left:* MARC FAIRBURN

*Top right:* JASON BUTCHER

*Above:* DAVID CORDEN

*Opposite:* HENNING JORGENSEN

# Dragons

Within the tattoo world, the dragon normally falls into two categories, the Western dragon and the Oriental dragon. The Western dragon is generally depicted as a flying, scaled, almost snake-like creature breathing fire. It is seen in fantasy-type pieces or 'George and the Dragon' tattoos. The elaborate Oriental dragon design, either malevolent or benevolent, is a much-favoured theme in Japanese tattooing, the images often covering large areas of skin.

Top left: DAVE BRYANT

Middle left: IAN FLOWER

Bottom left: GEORGE BONE

Above: STEFF REIDER

Left: HENNING JORGENSEN

Below: HENNING JORGENSEN

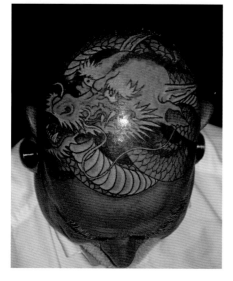

*Top left:* IAN FLOWER

*Top centre:* GEORGE BONE

*Top right:* HENNING JORGENSEN

*Left:* GEORGE BONE

*Above:* RHYS GORDON

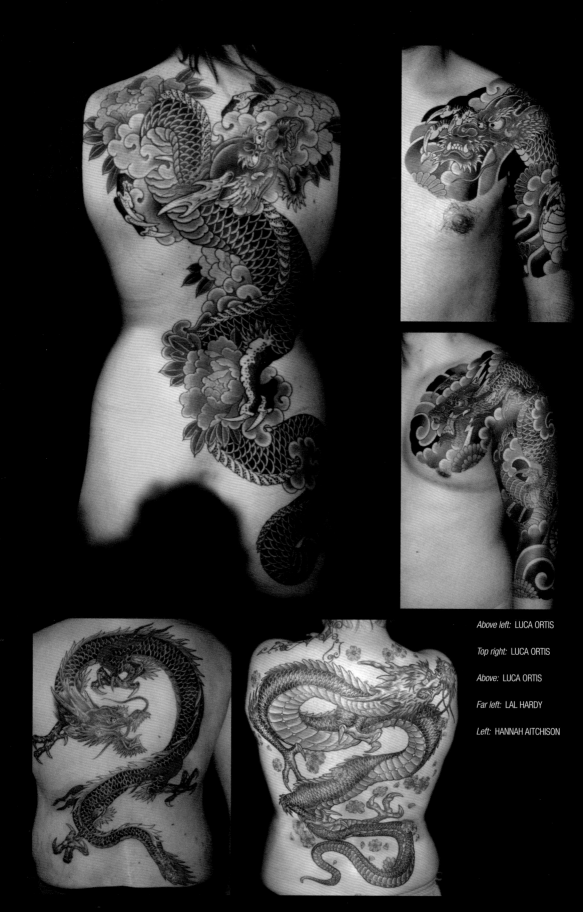

*Above left:* LUCA ORTIS

*Top right:* LUCA ORTIS

*Above:* LUCA ORTIS

*Far left:* LAL HARDY

*Left:* HANNAH AITCHISON

Top left: HANNAH AITCHISON

Top right: HENNING JORGENSEN

Left: STEWART ROBSON

Above: MARK B

# Mermaids

These mythical aquatic creatures, half-woman, half-fish (or, in the case case of mermen, half-man, half-fish) are very popular tattoos. The mermaid, or siren, is said to have lured many a sailor to his watery grave.

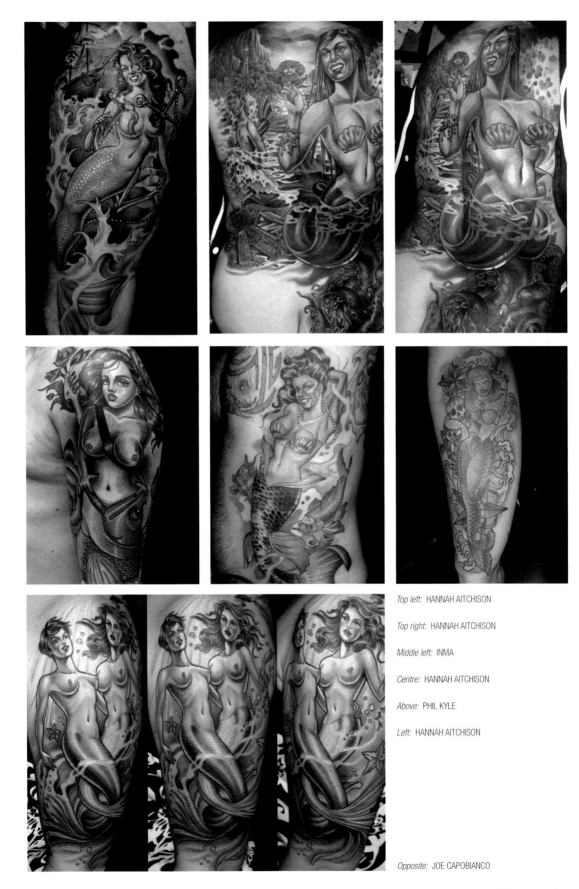

*Top left:* HANNAH AITCHISON

*Top right:* HANNAH AITCHISON

*Middle left:* INMA

*Centre:* HANNAH AITCHISON

*Above:* PHIL KYLE

*Left:* HANNAH AITCHISON

*Opposite:* JOE CAPOBIANCO

# HARDWARE & WARFARE

**M**ore and more we see mechanical images such as clocks, compasses, engines, guns, motorcyles, automobiles and assorted items of machinery being used as skin illustrations, some even showing what appear to be robotic body parts.

# Military

Soldiers, sailors and airmen have always been associated with tattooing. Sailors or soldiers in a foriegn land were regulars at the local tattoo studios where personnel alighting ships for leave would often spend their wages in the bars, brothels and tattoo shops – hence the saying 'stewed, screwed and tattooed'!

*Top:* GENTLEMAN JIM

*Left:* LAL HARDY

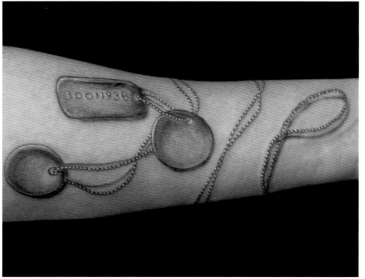

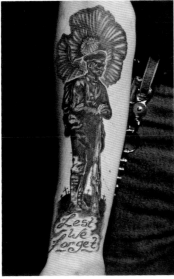

*Top left:* LAL HARDY

*Top middle:* LAL HARDY

*Top right:* LAL HARDY

*Middle left:* DAN MARSHALL

*Centre:* MARTIN CLARK

*Above:* KIRSTY SIMPSON

*Far left:* LAL HARDY

*Left:* MICHAEL ROSE

Top left: STEFF REIDER

Middle left: DARREN STARES

Left: WAYNE GRACE

Top right: HANNAH AITCHISON

Above: LAL HARDY

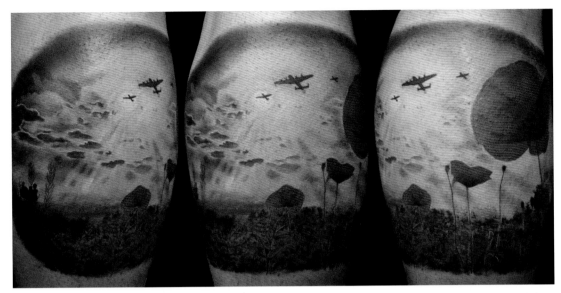

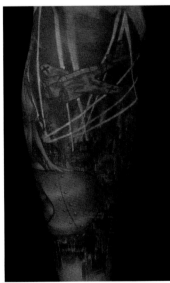

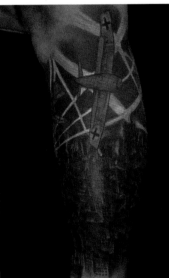

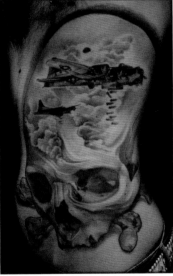

*Top:* DAVID CORDEN

*Above left:* ROB DOUBTFIRE

*Above right:* JASON BUTCHER

*Right:* CECIL PORTER

*Far right:* MARK GIBSON

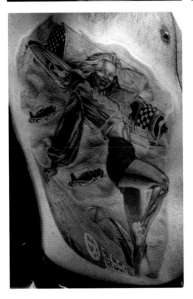

# Warriors

The fascination with ancient military history and fighting men is often reflected in tattooing with samurai , gladiators and vikings all being popular choices of design.

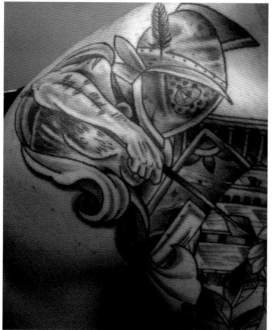

*Top left:* MARK THE SHARK

*Top middle:* LAL HARDY

*Top right:* MICK TOMO

*Far left:* DAN MARSHALL

*Left:* CHANCE KENTON

*Below:* LIORCIFER


*Opposite page*

*Top:* CHANCE KENTON

*Bottom:* CHANCE KENTON

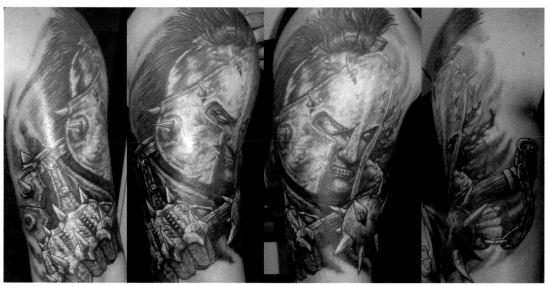

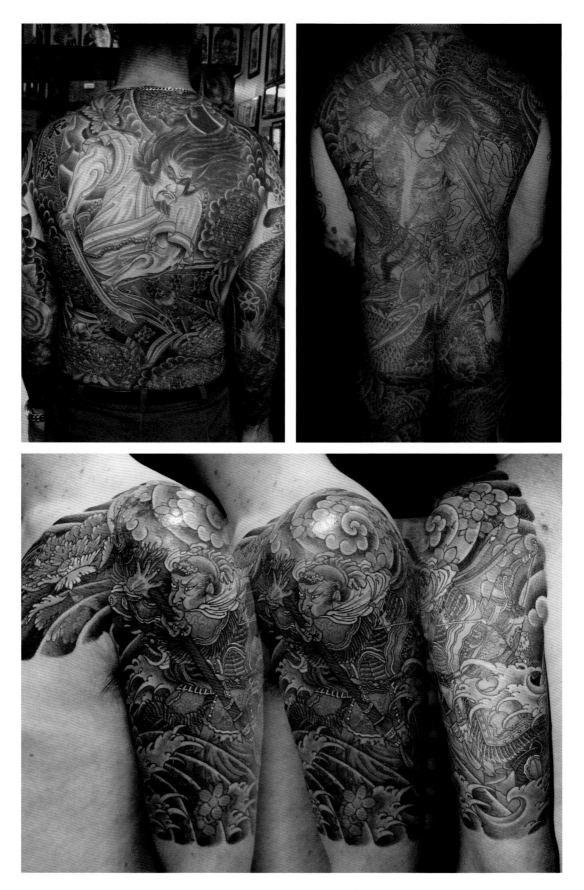

*Above left:* MARK GIBSON

*Above right:* RON KOUPAL

*Right:* MATT BUTLER

*Opposite page*

*Top left:* MATT BUTLER

*Top right:* HENNING JORGENSEN

*Bottom:* STEWART ROBSON

# Machines

I find it fascinating that so many people choose machine-based tattoo images now and often it is a tribute to the skill of the artist that they can tattoo such diverse machines as cars and typewriters.

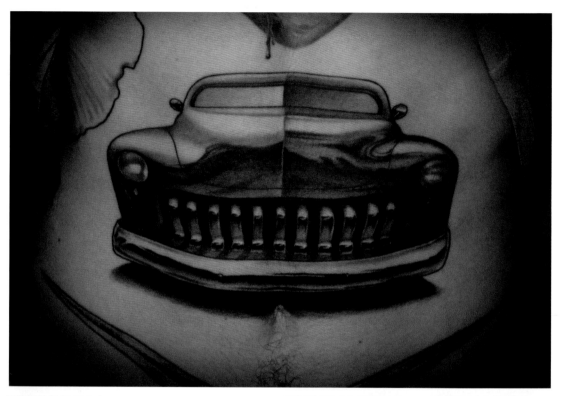

Top: TIM HENDRICKS

Left: MARK B

Above left: MARK B

Above right: JASON BUTCHER

Opposite page
Top left: ADAM COLLINS

Top right: STEFF REIDER

Second right: ROB DOUBTFIRE

Right: MARK THE SHARK

Far right: RODNEY RAINES

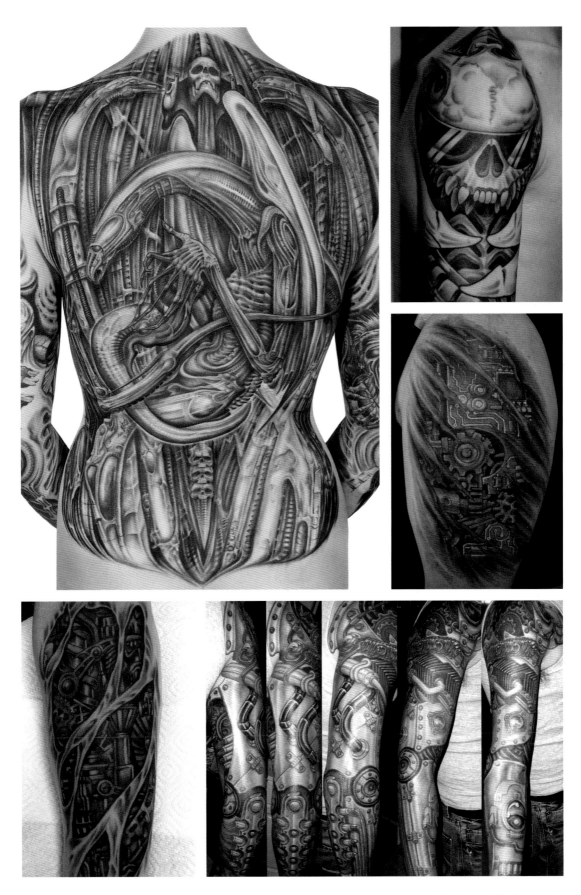

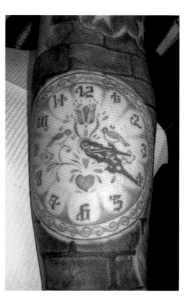

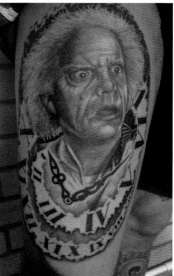

*Top left:* MARK B

*Top centre:* TRACY @ HAUNTED

*Top right:* LAL HARDY

*Middle left:* MARK GIBSON

*Centre:* MARK GIBSON

*Above:* LEIGH OLDCORN

*Far left:* LAL HARDY

*Left:* RODNEY RAINES

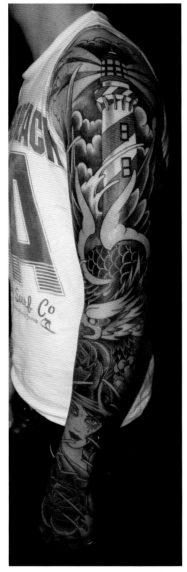

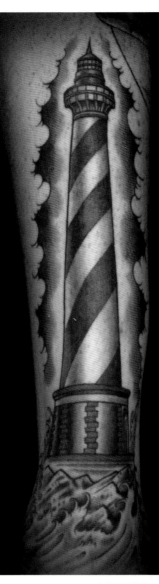

Above left: PAUL SCARROTT

Centre: TIM HENDRICKS

Right: TIMY MISS BECCA

Top right: PHIL YOUNG

Middle right: LAL HARDY

Bottom right: TIM HENDRICKS

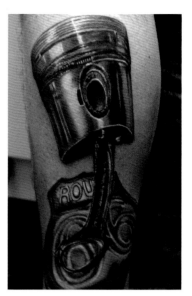

*Top left:* KEVIN PAUL

*Above middle:* MARK GIBSON

*Above:* CECIL PORTER

*Far left:* MARK B

*Left:* MARK GIBSON

*Below left:* JOE CAPOBIANCO

*Below:* CHRISTIAN PEREZ

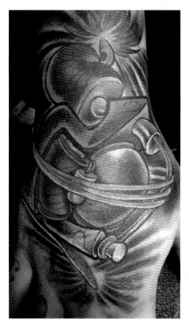
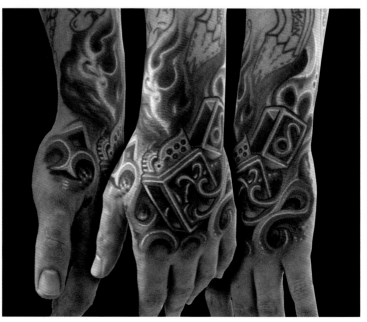

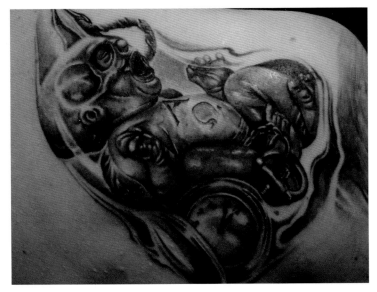

*Top left:* JASON BUTCHER

*Above:* JAMES CUMBERLAND

*Far left:* MARK GIBSON

*Left:* JASON VAUGHAN

*Below left:* PHIL KYLE

*Below middle:* MARK GIBSON

*Below:* PHIL KYLE

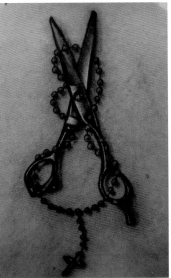

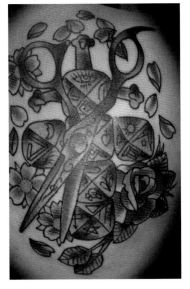

# Ships

No design captures the nautical flavour of tattooing more than the iconic image of a tall ship or galleon fully rigged, sails billowing, flags flying as it tops a wave.

*Top left:* DAVE BRYANT

*Bottom left:* ADRIAN WILLARD

*Above:* JASON VAUGHAN

*Below:* INMA

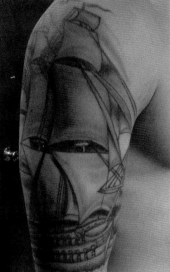

*Top left:* STEFANO CERA

*Top right:* STEFANO CERA

*Above left:* TOM WELLS

*Centre:* PHIL KYLE

*Above right:* ERIC MERRILL

*Right:* WIL PURNELL

# Guns

The gun has, in recent tattoo history, become a very popular design, whether it be the fancy, decorated six-shooters of the wild west, the highwayman's flintlock or the Uzis and AK-47s of the present day.

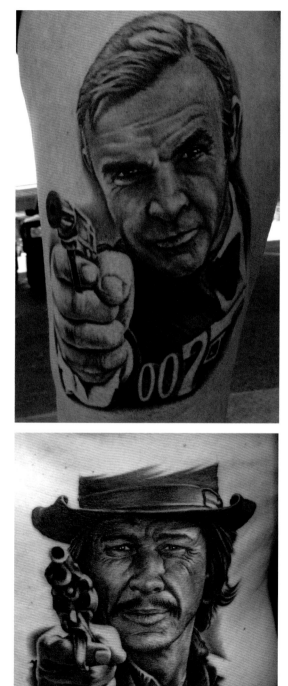

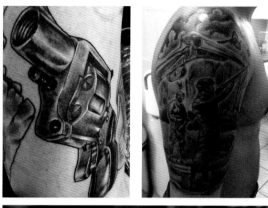

Top left: BOB TYRRELL

Bottom left: BOB TYRRELL

Top centre: DAN ROOKE

Top right: MICK TOMO

Second right: JOHN ANDERTON

Above: NATE DREW

Left: MARK THE SHARK

*Left:* STEFF REIDER

*Above:* DAVID CORDEN

*Below left:* MATT PERRY

*Below right:* LEIGH OLDCORN

*Bottom left:* MARK GIBSON

*Bottom right:* MATT PERRY

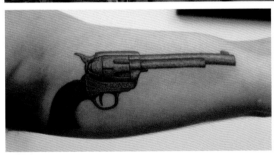

# FOOD OF LOVE

What tattoo volume would be complete without a section dedicated to the elements that comprise the food of love?

# Music

It is hard to imagine a world without music. Music that can convey every emotion, music that makes us dance, sing, laugh and cry. It is no wonder so many people celebrate music through their tattoos, be it a favourite singer's portrait, an instrument or a line from a particular song.

*Top left:* JOHN ANDERTON

*Top centre:* JULIO RODRIGUEZ

*Top right:* JASON BUTCHER

*Above:* LAL HARDY

*Centre:* HANNAH AITCHISON

*Above right:* DAVID CORDEN

*Right:* TIM HENDRICKS

*Far right:* JOHN ANDERTON

*Opposite page*

*Top:* LIANNE MOULE

*Bottom:* JASON VAUGHAN

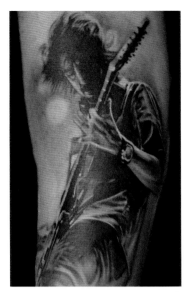

Above: JASON BUTCHER

Right: CHRISTIAN PEREZ

Below left: STEVE A

Below centre: GEORGE BONE

Below right: JOHN ANDERTON

Opposite page
Top left: STEFF REIDER

Top centre: DAVE BRYANT

Top right: INMA

Middle left: CECIL PORTER

Centre: MICK TOMO

Middle right: LUCI LOU

Bottom left: MICK J

Bottom centre: SONYA TRUSTY

Bottom right: MARTIN CLARK

Top left: DARRYLL RICHARDS

Top right: ADAM COLLINS

Bottom left: DARRYLL RICHARDS

Bottom right: MARK GIBSON

*Above:* LIORCIFER

*Right:* LAL HARDY

# Romance

Love – that emotion that can captivate us all – is often manifested through tattoos and these often feature the name of a lover, but this has led to an old adage within the tattoo trade – 'tattoos last longer than romances'!

*Above:* JULIO RODRIGUEZ

*Right:* VALERIE VARGAS

*Opposite:* KORE FLATMO

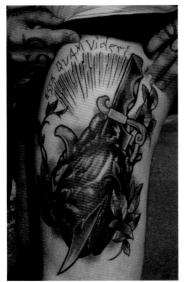

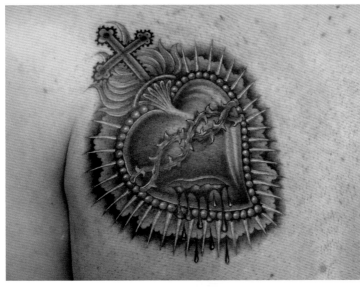

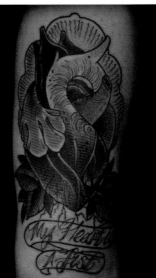

*Top left:* TOM WELLS

*Top centre:* TRACY @ HAUNTED

*Top right:* MARK GIBSON

*Middle left:* VALERIE VARGAS

*Above:* MARK B

*Far left:* NARESH BHANA

*Left:* TINY MISS BECCA

Opposite page
*Top:* NATE DREW

*Bottom left:* VALERIE VARGAS

*Bottom right:* TINY MISS BECCA

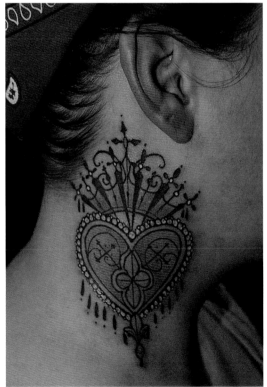

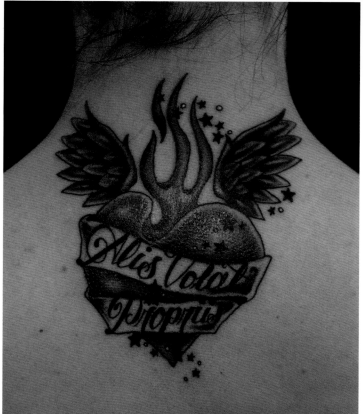

Top: KELLEY DRAKE

Right: GEMMA KAHLUA

Opposite: MARK B

# Trees and Branches

The tree of life, family trees and mighty oaks are all found in the tattoo forest.

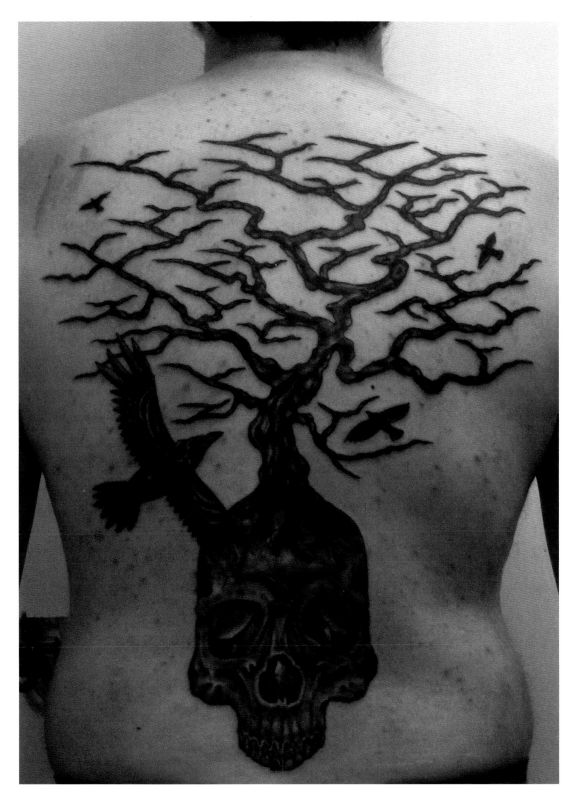

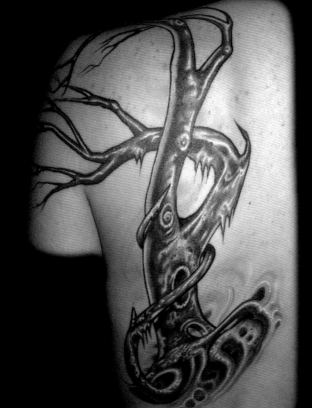

*Above left:* CHRISTIAN PEREZ

*Above:* KELLEY DRAKE

*Left:* CHRISTIAN PEREZ

*Opposite page*
*Top left:* DARRYLL RICHARDS

*Top right:* CURLY

*Bottom:* LAL HARDY

*Above:* PHIL YOUNG

*Above right:* GEMMA KAHLUA

*Right:* SAM JONES

*Opposite:* MARK B

# Food and Drink

A modern day phenomenon is the vast array of food and drink tattoos. You can find everything from your favourite tipple to ultra realistic sundaes or mouthwatering burgers. They can all be enjoyed through a tattoo needle with the bonus of zero calories !

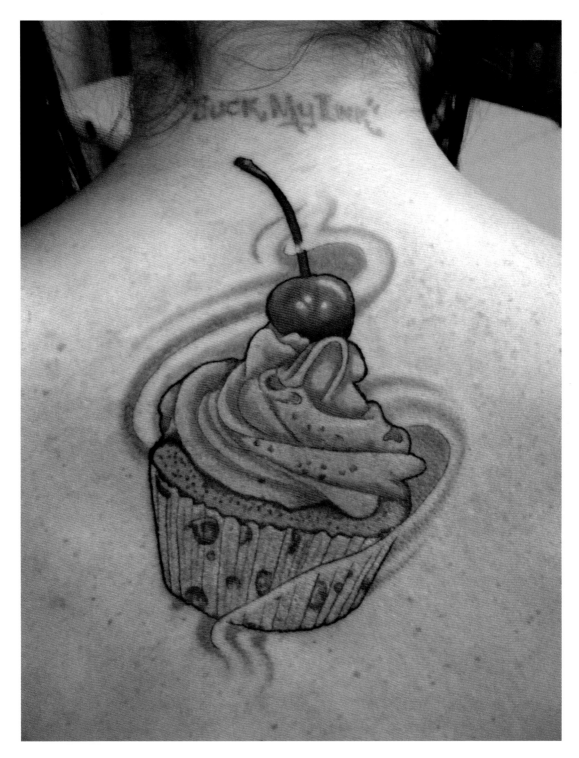

*Above left:* STEFF REIDER

*Above centre:* ANDREW ZELENA @ HAUNTED

*Above:* GENTLEMAN JIM

*Left:* NICK SKUNX

*Below left:* CHRISTIAN PEREZ

*Below right:* CHRISTIAN PEREZ

*Above:* KELLEY DRAKE

*Above centre:* JOHN ANDERTON

*Above right:* LEIGH OLDCORN

*Right:* WIL PURNELL

*Far right:* TOR ABYSS

*Below:* MIREK VEL STOTKER

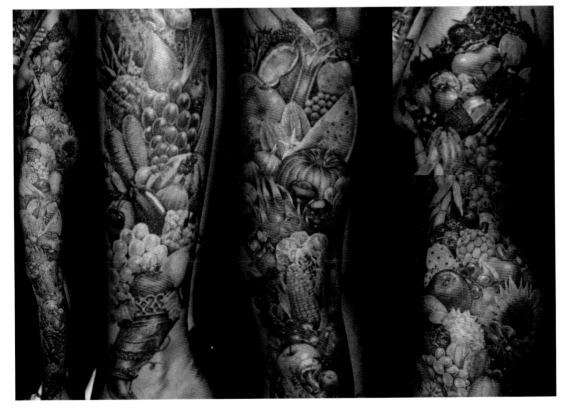

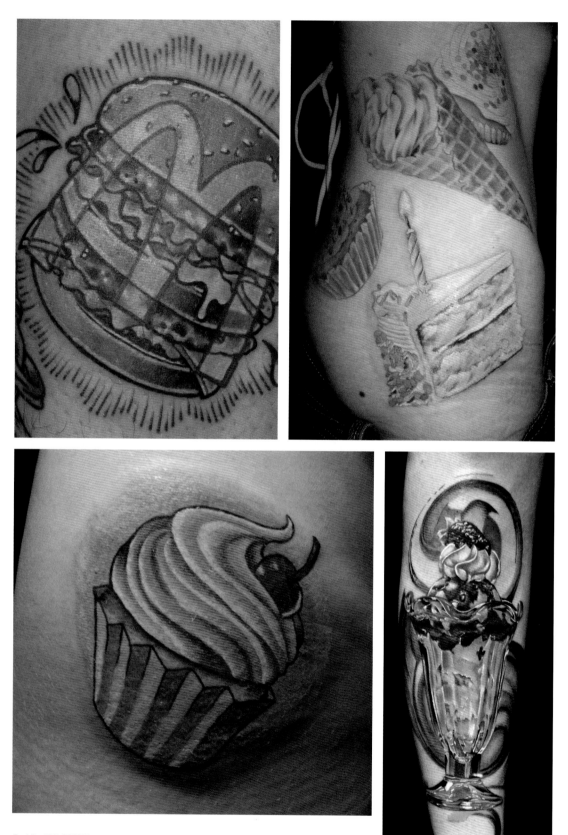

*Top left:* JULIA SEIZURE

*Bottom left:* SAM JONES

*Top right:* PAUL SCARROTT

*Bottom right:* CECIL PORTER

Above: TOR ABYSS

Above centre: INMA

Above right: JULIA SEIZURE

Right: PHIL YOUNG

Far right: WAYNE GRACE

Below left: ADAM COLLINS

Below centre: VALERIE VARGAS

Below right: MARTIN CLARK

# Flowers

The beauty of nature is wonderfully expressed through the incredible diversity of flowers found throughout the world. Flowers symbolize so many things – the red rose of love, the lily of death, the secret love of acacia, the daisy of innocence. It is only natural that with so many flowers of so many colours they have become a mainstay of tattooing.

*Above:* MARK GIBSON

*Right:* MARK B

*Below left:* SONYA TRUSTY

*Below centre:* PIOTREK TATON

*Below right:* LIANNE MOULE

*Opposite:* CALYPSO SAGA

*Above left:* INMA

*Above:* LIANNE MOULE

*Far left:* TOM WELLS

*Left:* SILVIA Z

*Below left:* LIANNE MOULE

*Below:* MARK THE SHARK

*Opposite page*

*Top left:* MICK TOMO

*Middle left:* LAL HARDY

*Bottom left:* PHIL YOUNG

*Top right:* HARRY O

*Below centre:* PHIL YOUNG

*Below right:* PHIL YOUNG

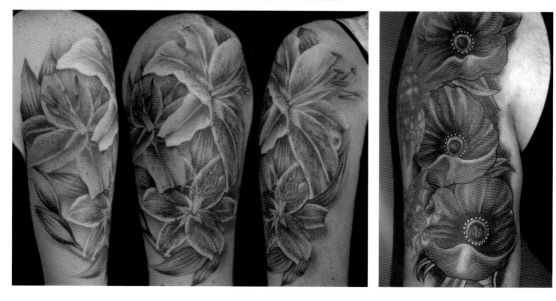

A
ANDERTON, JOHN www.nemesistattoo.co.uk
AITCHISON, HANNAH www.hannahaitchison.com
B
BONE, GEORGE www.georgebonetattoos.co.uk
BHANA, NARESH www.flamineight.co.uk
BINNIE, ALEX www.alexbinnie.com
www.into-you.co.uk
BLACK, MATT mattblacktattoo.wordpress.com
BROWN, KENNY www.jbtrtattoo.com
BLAKELEY, GEMMA www.myspace.com/electrikink
BRYANT, DAVE www.evilfromtheneedle.com
BUTCHER, JASON www.immortalink.co.uk
BUTLER, MATT www.mrbutlertattoos.com
C
CALYPSO www.into-you.co.uk
CAPOBIANCO, JOE www.hopegallerytattoo.com
CERA, STEFANO weakbecomeheroes.com
frithstreettattoo.co.uk
CLARK, MARTIN www.bluebirdtattoo.co.uk
COLLINS, ADAM www.adamtattoo.com
www.newwavetattoo.co.uk
CORDEN, DAVID www.davidcordentattoos.com
www.ritual-art-tattoo.com
CURLY www.tattoocurly.com
CUMBERLAND, JAMES www.jamescumberland.com
D
DONE, BOB www.magnumopustattoo.com
DOUBTFIRE, ROB www.robstattoostudio.co.uk
DRAKE, KELLEY www.jbtrtattoo.com
DREW, NATE www.jbtrtattoo.com
E
ELY SMYLY www.flamineight.co.uk
ERL, SIMON simonerl.tumblr.com
F
FAIRBURN, MARC www.scribbleinktattoo.co.uk
FLATMO, KORE www.plurabella.com
FLOWER, IAN www.newskooltattoos.co.uk
G
GORDON, RHYS www.rhysgordon.com
www.tatudharma.com
GRACE, WAYNE gracetattoo.co.uk
www.newwavetattoo.co.uk
GRAVES, ALLAN hauntedcustomtattoos.blogspot.com
GENTLEMAN, JIM gentlemanjimtattoos.com
H
HALL, DAVE www.kustomkulture.co.uk
HARDY, LAL www.lalhardyink.co.uk
www.newwavetattoo.co.uk
HARRIS, TIM www.hopegallerytattoo.com
HAUNTED, TOR (Abyss) hauntedcustomtattoos.blogspot.com
HAUNTED, TRACEY hauntedcustomtattoos.blogspot.com
HAUNTED, ANDREW (Zelena) hauntedcustomtattoos.blogspot.com
HENDRICKS, TIM saltwatertattoo.com
HUNJAN, SAIRA ilovegoodtimes.co.uk
HIGGINS, CHRIS www.chrishigginstattoo.co.uk
www.into-you.co.uk
HORN, NICK nickhorn.wordpress.com
I
INNIT, CLAIRE www.claireinnit.co.uk
INMA www.inmatattooartist.com
www.thefamilybusinesstattoo.com
J
JOHNSON, RAY www.rayjohnsonuk.com
www.immortalink.co.uk
JULES www.inkerstattoo.co.uk
JONES, SAM www.robstattoostudio.co.uk
JORGENSEN, HENNING www.royaltattoo.com
K
KING, JAMES www.flamineight.co.uk
KENYON, CHANCE www.jbtrtattoo.com
KOUPAL, RON www.royaltattoo.com
KYLE, PHIL www.magnumopustattoo.com
philkyle.tumblr.com

L
LIORCIFER www.liorcifer.com
tribulationtattoo.com
LUCI LOU www.lucizz.com
www.magnumopustattoo.com
LOWE, NIKOLE ilovegoodtimes.co.uk
LYNN, AKURA www.magnumopustattoo.com
M
MARK B www.suckmyink.com
MARK "the" SHARK www.facebook.com/thirteenink
MARSHALL, DAN tribulationtattoo.com
MERRILL, ERIC www.hopegallerytattoo.com
MICK, J www.bluedragontattoo.co.uk
MOULE, LIANNE www.immortalink.co.uk
O
O, HARRY www.flamineight.co.uk
OLDCORN, LEIGH www.cosmictattoo.com
ORTIS, LUCA www.lucaortis.com
www.newwavetattoo.co.uk
P
PAUL, KEVIN www.facebook.com/kevinpaultattoo
PEREZ, CHRISTIAN www.hopegallerytattoo.com
PERRY, MATT www.bluedragontattoo.co.uk
PORTER, CECIL www.cecilportertattoos.com
PRYOR, LUCY www.lucypryor.com
www.into-you.co.uk
PURNELL, WILL www.facebook.com/blacktidestattoo
R
RAINES, RODNEY www.acecustomtattoo.com
REID, CLAIRE www.clairereid.net
RICHARDS, DARRYLL www.mantratattoo.com
REIDER, STEFF www.thetattooedarm.com
ROBSON, STEWART www.stewartrobson.com
frithstreettattoo.co.uk
RODRIGUEZ, JULIO www.hopegallerytattoo.com
ROOKE, DAN www.facebook.com/pages/rookstar-tattoo
ROSE, MICHAEL www.michaelrosevisualart.com
S
SCARROTT, PAUL www.mantratattoo.com
SEIZURE, JULIA www.juliaseizure.com
www.flamineight.co.uk
SIMPSON, KIRSTY www.robstattoostudio.co.uk
SKUNX, NICK www.skunxtattoo.com
SOFFE, AARON www.bluedragontattoo.co.uk
STARES, DARREN www.staresy.com
STEVE A www.steve-a.co.uk
STOTKER, vel MIREK www.stotkertattoo.com
T
TALBOT, JO www.facebook.com/thirteenink
TAS tastattooing.wordpress.com
www.into-you.co.uk
TATON, PIOTREK ilovegoodtimes.co.uk
TINY MISS BECCA www.jaynedoetattoo.com
TOMAS, TOMAS www.siddhamrastu.co.uk
tomastomas108.wordpress.com
TOMO, MICK www.micktomo.com
TRITTEN, JASON hartandhuntington.com
TRUSTY, SONYA www.redstattoo.co.uk
TYRRELL, BOB www.bobtyrrell.com
V
VARGAS, VALERIE valerievargas.com
frithstreettattoo.co.uk
VAUGHAN, JASON jasonvaughntattoos.com
W
WELLS, TOM www.facebook.com/twellstattoo
WILLARD, ADRIAN www.magnumopustattoo.com
X
DUNCAN X www.duncanx.com
www.into-you.co.uk
Y
YOUNG, PHIL www.philyoungtattoos.com
www.hopegallerytattoo.com
Z
ZED, SILVIA www.facebook.com/silviazed
www.newwavetattoo.co.uk